CROSSING THE SEA

WITH SYRIANS ON THE EXODUS TO EUROPE

Wolfgang Bauer

PHOTOS BY
Stanislav Krupař

TRANSLATED BY
Sarah Pybus

other stories

LOS ANGELES · HIGH WYCOMBE

ISBN 9781908276827
eBook ISBN 9781908276834

A catalogue record for this book is available from the British Library.

Editor: Stefan Tobler; Typesetter: Tetragon, London; Typefaces: Linotype
Swift Neue, Verlag; Cover Design: Edward Bettison. Printed and bound by
the CPI Group (UK) Ltd, Croydon, CRO 4YY.

And Other Stories is supported by public funding from Arts Council
England.

The translation of this work was supported by a grant from the Goethe-
Institut, which is funded by the German Ministry of Foreign Affairs.

Supported using public funding by
**ARTS COUNCIL
ENGLAND**

**GOETHE
INSTITUT**

CROSSING
THE SEA

PART ONE

THE BEACH I

'Run!' The high voice of a young man, a child still really, yells behind me. 'Run!' I start to run without fully understanding what's going on; without seeing much in the dusk, we run single-file down the narrow path. I run as fast as I can, watching my feet land now on dirt and now on rock. I jump over holes in the ground, over chunks of wall, stumble and keep going. 'You sons of bitches!' The shout comes from one of the boys who have just driven us out of the minibuses and now run alongside us, whacking us like cattle hands driving their herds. He beats us with a stick, hitting our backs and legs. He grabs my arm, cursing as he pulls me forwards. There are fifty-nine of us – men, women and children, whole families – with rucksacks on our backs and cases in our hands, running down a long factory wall somewhere on the edge of an industrial zone in Alexandria, Egypt.

In front of me, Hussan's back rises and falls. A bulky twenty-year-old, eyes to the ground, wheezes, soon begins to stagger, blocks my way because he can't go on, stops suddenly, so I push him on from behind, I push with all my strength until he starts running again. Blows rain down on us. Somewhere in front of Hussan, thirteen-year-old Bissan cries with fear. As she runs, she clings to the rucksack containing her diabetes medication. 'Scum!' shouts the man driving us forwards. Behind me, fifty-year-old Amar wears the highly visible, signal-blue Gore-Tex jacket he bought specially for this day; his daughter thought the colour was stylish. He too gets slower and slower; his knee hurts, his back too, but as he said earlier, he's going to make it. He has to make it. Like almost everyone here, he comes from Syria. For him, Egypt is just one stop on his journey. Then the wall turns sharply to the left and suddenly, not even fifty metres away, we see what we have been anticipating and fearing for days. The sea. Glistening before us in the last of the evening light.

In April 2014, photographer Stanislav Krupař and I joined a group of Syrian refugees trying to get across the sea from Egypt to Italy. We put ourselves in the hands of people smugglers who have no idea that we are journalists. That's why we get herded forward with sticks like the rest; we all need to move quickly so our large group doesn't attract attention. They would never take journalists along for fear of being betrayed to the security services. This is the most dangerous aspect of our journey: being unmasked by the smugglers. Only Amar and his family know who we really are. He is an old friend from my time reporting on the Syrian civil war. It was desperation that drove him here; he dreams of living in Germany. He will translate and interpret for us along the way. We have grown long beards and adopted new identities. For this journey, we are English teachers Varj and Servat, two refugees from a republic in the Caucasus.

We are now part of the great exodus. In 2014, according to the United Nations High Commissioner for Refugees (UNHCR), 207,000 people fled across the Mediterranean to Europe, most of them starting from Libya. In the whole year before that, it was only 60,000. They come from war-ravaged countries such as Syria and Somalia, from dictatorships like Eritrea, or in search of a life under better economic conditions.

The political order of the Middle East is collapsing. Decades of subjugation have built up immense social tensions that are now erupting into violence. Dictatorships are falling, as are the democratically elected governments that followed them. Cairo's streets are filled with bloody demonstrations. Yemen is descending into chaos, Iraq too. Libya has splintered into regions where the militia fight amongst themselves. But no country has experienced such utter destruction as Syria, on a scale not seen since the Vietnam War and Chechnya. Cities are lunar landscapes. Many villages are all but abandoned. For three years now, Bashar al-Assad has been waging a war of annihilation with every weapon at his disposal, including chemical agents. Alawites fight Sunnis, and no one side can gain the upper hand. And to add to it all, religious extremists preaching a creed of hatred have carved out a space for themselves in this chaos.

Syria's horrors can no longer be grasped in statistics. The UN stopped counting the dead in early 2014.

Attempts to escape the danger are also becoming increasingly perilous. Every year, 1,500 people drown as they flee to Italy and Greece. This figure is probably much higher, but the corpses are never found. Smugglers are choosing ever riskier routes as the continent improves measures to seal its borders. 400,000 police officers stand guard. Europe has built six-metre-high fences such as those in the Spanish exclaves of Melilla and Ceuta. Bulgaria and Greece have also erected structures to protect against refugees. Europe has installed elaborate radar and camera systems in the Strait of Gibraltar. The Atlantic Ocean is also being monitored between the Canaries and West Africa. Police forces, soldiers and elite units from various nations have become embroiled in the defensive battle.

Helicopters, drones and a fleet of warships are being deployed. With this many troops and so much equipment, you might think they were fighting a military invasion.

And so, once again, Europe's borders become death strips.

Over five decades, 125 refugees were killed at the Berlin Wall in the GDR, for which the free world denounced it as a symbol of inhumanity. By the time of our trip in early 2014, almost 20,000 refugees have lost their lives at the walls with which Europe surrounded itself after the Cold War. Most of them have drowned in the Mediterranean. No sea border in the world has claimed so many lives.

Europe's birthplace, the Mediterranean has now become the setting of its greatest failure.

No other journalists have dared take a boat from Egypt, and we are aware of the dangers. We each carry a satellite phone to notify the Italian coastguard in an emergency. We decided against setting out from Libya or Tunisia. Although both are closer to Italy, the boats used there are extremely rickety. Egyptian smugglers have to cover a larger distance, so they use better ships. At least that was our hope. We were naive. We thought the sea would be the greatest hazard. In fact, it was just one of many.

FAREWELL I

One week before we are beaten with sticks and herded to the shore, Amar Obaid (not his real name) stands indecisively in his Cairo apartment.* It is Tuesday 8 April, his last day with his family. His seventeen-year-old daughter Reynala sits on the edge of her parents' bed and looks at her father. 'What should I take with me?' he asks, standing before the open wardrobe with his hands on his hips. He can't take much. Amar has heard that the people smugglers accept only hand luggage, no heavy suitcases. 'Warm underwear to protect against the wind out at sea,' says his daughter. 'A good shirt,' says Amar. 'I don't want to look like a crook in Italy.' 'You will anyway,' she says, 'you'll grow a long grey beard.' 'The life jacket,' he says, stripping it from its packaging and deliberately putting it on the wrong way round. His daughter laughs and he laughs, does a little twirl for her. Their shared laughter echoes through the apartment.

A 280-square-metre living room in the baroque style, with magnificent gold-printed wallpaper and sprawling sofas. Originally from Homs in Syria, this well-to-do family has been part of the merchant and landowner class for generations. But after the revolution broke out in 2011, Amar, his wife and their three daughters fled to Egypt.

---

* Unless referring to public figures, the names of those involved have been changed. Biographical details have also been altered slightly.

Like many of his clan, he had previously joined the resistance against Assad. To stay would have been to risk both his life and the lives of his family. He took his savings and set up a small import business in Cairo, bringing in furniture from Bali and India. He opened a shop, which employed up to eight people at its height, and travelled a lot. But then Egypt plunged into first a revolution and then a counter-revolution, as the military overthrew the democratically elected president, Mohamed Morsi. In just a few months, public opinion turned against the Syrian refugees. The junta imposed visa requirements and Amar was no longer able to leave the country for business trips. He was afraid of being denied an entry visa.

Xenophobia starts to spread along the Nile. TV presenters preach hatred of Syrians, who struggle to find work. Egyptians urge others to stop buying from Syrian retailers such as Amar. Many Egyptians regard Syrians as destabilising terrorists, as freeloaders who take their jobs.

Egypt has turned out to be a trap for the fleeing family. They cannot return to Syria and have no future here.

After long discussion, the family decides to flee again. To Germany. There is no legal way to do it. They decide that Amar will go first. As soon as he has been granted asylum, he will fetch the rest of the family. At least that's what they have planned here, in their living room, amongst the sofa cushions. It is an optimistic plan, but not impossible. They know that, despite the dangers, most boats make it across. And once he reaches Sicily, there is actually a good chance of getting to Germany undiscovered. Amar's hope is that, like many Syrians before him, he will in all probability be recognised as an asylum seeker. The only thing standing between his family and a better future is the sea.

'How long will the boat take?' asks his wife Rolanda. 'I don't know exactly,' Amar replies on their last evening. He might be on the boat for five days; it might be three weeks. He has heard so many different stories about the crossing.

Rolanda stays up late smoking an e-cigarette. Amar's wife wears skin-tight black latex trousers. Gradually, his family gather around him. His youngest child, just five years old, snuggles into the crook of her mother's arm as she eats. She instinctively avoids her father, turns away from him. She is hurt that he is leaving, even if she cannot comprehend the dangers his journey will hold. The second-youngest, a thirteen-year-old with braces, her voice rough from a cold, doesn't want to leave Cairo. She is the only one who wants to stay in Egypt. Her friends are here, her favourite cafés – she has nothing in Germany. In contrast, the eldest girl declares 'Heaven – Germany!' on her Facebook page. She wants to study psychology in Germany. She begged her father to take her with him, but he said no because she is not yet eighteen. 'She takes after me the most,' says Amar. Both girls attend an international school whose fees take up half the family's budget.

His mother-in-law and her servant appear at the table, the setting for their last evening meal together. The grande dame of the family, who also fled from Homs, drinks her tea with her little finger extended. She says crossing the sea is too demeaning, too risky. He is jeopardising the entire family's future. 'What will happen to my daughter, your wife, if you come to a watery end?' she asks. Throughout the evening, his mother-in-law struggles to retain her composure. The servant prepares the food in the kitchen and helps Amar's wife; she doesn't agree with it either. She has tears in her eyes. Their cousin is at the table too; he's a diamond merchant from

Homs who will soon be leaving Egypt – for Homs. 'I have nothing to fear from the Syrian government. I've been trying to get a trading licence in Egypt for half a year now, without success.' He wants to try his luck again in Syria, where the diamond trade is booming. They are the perfect investment during a civil war: tiny stones of enormous value that are easy to conceal.

The family eats together one last time; the women have spent a long time in the kitchen. The men make a valiant effort to tell jokes, but most of the time they sit at the table with their heads bowed.

'So who bought the shop?' their cousin asks. 'My accountant,' says Amar. 'For a quarter of its true price. He's promised to keep on both of my employees.' 'I hope you've made the right decision,' his cousin says. Amar looks down at the table.

He has spent today paying and calling in the last of his invoices. The family has enough money saved to survive for half a year without him.

Amar spends the last hours of his old life in fitful sleep. He must cast aside everything he once was: a father, a businessman who solved problems over the phone. He will spend the next few months as a refugee, nothing more. It's as though his life has been reset.

The next morning, as they say goodbye at the door, Rolanda hugs him, cries and pulls him to her. 'Oh God,' she says. 'I miss you already.' He breaks away from her quickly, almost roughly, so that he doesn't change his mind. He hurries through the door without looking back. He promised himself he wouldn't cry. He wants to show his family that he has his destiny under control. Everything will be OK, he tells himself over and over, I have a plan. His eldest daughter follows him to the car, carrying his rucksack. He hugs her briefly and gives her a smile. My strong, beautiful daughter. She cries, although she had also resolved not to. He slams the door and pulls out of the parking space, his hands shaking.

At best, it will be months before Amar sees his wife and children again. But it could be years. And if worst comes to worst: never.

FLEEING

In Egypt, people smuggling has a structure not dissimilar to the tourism industry. Sales points with 'agents' are spread throughout the country. These agents assure their customers that they work with only the best smugglers, when in reality they have contracts with just a few. The crossing costs around three thousand dollars. Cheaper and more expensive services are available, but ultimately all travel classes end up in the same boat. The agent receives a commission of about three hundred dollars. This is kept by a middleman until the passenger's safe arrival in Italy. The sales agents – well, most of them – care about their reputation. Their livelihood depends on recommendations from the people they have successfully helped across the water.

Amar's agent is called Nuri. An old acquaintance, muscular with a deep, raw voice, he also works in furniture imports. We share the same sense of humour, says Amar, who finds it comforting. This journey may be fraught with uncertainties, but Amar knows how to make Nuri laugh. Nuri laughs a lot. This raucous laugh, which bellows from Amar's smartphone, will accompany us from now on.

The motorway, Amar's route to a better future, is congested. We barely move; all five lanes are bumper to bumper, typical Cairo traffic. Amar curses, thumps the steering wheel, beeps the horn. He phones to tell Nuri we'll be late to the meeting point, a Kentucky Fried Chicken in 6th of October City, an industrial town thirty kilometres from downtown Cairo. 'I should have taken my sedative,' Amar grumbles. He has two types of pill with him – Seroxat, 20 milligrams, for depression and panic attacks, and Xanax, 0.25 milligrams, for anxiety. He has been suffering from a range of anxieties for a year now. The war in Syria and the crisis in Egypt have left their mark on Amar. Fear of bacteria, fear of radiation, fear of large crowds. Finally he reaches the meeting point. A young man, Nuri's colleague, squats in front of the fast-food outlet, smoking, his head bent over his smartphone. He has a ponytail and goatee; he nods and says that the driver will be here soon to take us to the coastal city of Alexandria, from where most refugee boats set sail for Italy.

'How are you?' Rolanda asks on the phone. 'Everything's fine,' he says. 'Did you pack your warm jacket?' she asks.

The man with the ponytail puffs on his cigarette and chuckles. We wait for hours. Amar tries to wheedle some details about the journey out of him, but the man gives nothing away. Three more passengers gather by the KFC: two brothers from Damascus, Alaa and Hussan, as we discover later, and their friend Bashar. They have brand-new sports rucksacks and black woolly hats. They are wary, and sit a little apart from us in a neighbouring café. It is getting dark by the time the minibus finally arrives, and we hurriedly load our rucksacks and cases. The driver doesn't say a word; he doesn't greet us and barely moves his head. Elias, a waiter from Hama with short hair and a glazed expression, is already sitting in the bus. The bus drives off and turns onto the main street. 'Shit,' barks the driver, suddenly breaking his silence.

'Only seven! Where are the others?'

He brakes and parks by the side of the road. He is nervous because the bus has an Alexandria number plate; if he stops for too long, people will notice. But then the latecomers arrive with their agent, Mohamed, foppish in a white peaked cap and shirt. Our paths will cross many times over the next few days. 'I'm sorry,' he says, shrugging. The driver yells at him. 'That's very unprofessional,' Amar complains, a true businessman. The two passengers say goodbye to their uncle, who brought them to the minibus. The new additions are Rabea and Asus, cousins from Syria, although they could hardly be more different. Rabea is fat and taciturn, Asus thin and talkative. Our group is now complete. Although we are suspicious of each other at first, the next few days will cement our friendship, our group, our only protection on this journey.

'I'm glad we found each other,' Alaa will say one night in the dark. 'As long as our group stays together, I have nothing to fear.'

The minibus continues its journey. Its passengers sit in silence with their bags on their laps, looking out of the windows. The Syrians stare out at a world they know so well and yet suddenly so little. For the first time, they are seeing what only those without papers see: the negative exposure of reality. White becomes black and black white. Since getting on this minibus, we have to avoid police checks. Some of the others have left their passports with friends in Cairo because they don't want to give their real names in Italy. They all want to continue on to Sweden or Germany. If they are registered in Italy, they will be forced to apply for asylum there.

The European Union's Dublin Regulation is what forces them to play this game of hide-and-seek. Germany in particular pushed for its introduction in Europe. It decrees that refugees must apply for asylum in the first EU country they enter. If they don't, if they press on to other countries – like Germany – they will be deported back to where they first set foot on European soil. In the centre

20

of Europe, Germany is surrounded almost exclusively by EU states. There is no way for potential asylum seekers to reach Germany directly – unless they fly. Everyone on the minibus wants to get to Italy, but none of them want to stay there. This is why they travel without papers. European bureaucracy ensures that here in Egypt the refugees are already highly vulnerable.

They all know the risks of travelling by water. They have heard of boats whose motors failed at sea, of boats that sank while still far from Italy. They have read about fraudsters who abandon their passengers off the coast of Tunisia, not Italy. They know refugees who have been arrested by the Egyptian coastguard or robbed on the beach by the smugglers, who injured themselves or even died when jumping from boats. But they also know of many who made it, who survived these terrifying days to reach Europe and never be afraid again.

In the meantime, night has fallen. The smuggler driving the minibus evades the police checkpoints on the main road to Alexandria by driving along unlit side streets. He often seems uncertain, asking at every crossroads which turn-off would be least dangerous. This area, which the police rarely patrol, is known for robberies and kidnappings. 'Is this road OK?' he asks a Bedouin at a crossing. 'No,' the man says without expression. 'That one is very unsafe.' A short time later, our path is blocked by a truck parked across the street. The driver is nervous, and pokes his head out of the side window. 'A hold-up?' asks Alaa, as the truck finally moves on.

Towering flames on either side, we are finally approaching Alexandria, an industrial Moloch with enormous refineries. This is Egypt's second-largest city, where six million people live on a narrow promontory between ocean and lagoon. They can't build outwards, so they build upwards. The concrete towers get bigger and bigger as they approach the sea, as if the city were one big sea defence, thirty floors high. Apartments fit together like honeycomb, a few in the light, most in the shade. Only the narrowest of streets remain between these gigantic constructions, like fissures in rock.

The minibus takes us deeper and deeper into the city.

As before, the driver provides no explanations, leaves us in the dark. He talks on the phone, telling some unknown person he's in such-and-such a place, taking this or that turning. Suddenly he dumps us by a café, in a crowd of gawping patrons. There's a Champions League match on the TV. Shortly after, a second minibus picks us up. This perplexing exercise is designed to shake off any police on our tail. 'Congratulations,' Nuri tells Amar on the phone. 'You'll be put on a boat tonight.' Our new bus heads into a dark alley. The driver, as tight-lipped as the first, turns off the engine. He calls to us to be quiet and keep our hands inside the vehicle. He gets out, pretends to clean the bus and waits. 'What's happening?' Amar asks in the dark. Nobody responds, and nobody dares ask the driver.

'We have to call it off,' Nuri explains by phone a little later. 'An hour ago the coastguard arrested a hundred refugees. We need to revise our plans.'

'Get out,' the driver snaps. It's four in the morning. He stops between inner-city skyscrapers, in a street empty at this time of day. Suddenly, light spills into the alley from one of the many entrances. A door opens, we hurry up the stairwell and an apartment door opens on one of the upper floors. We catch a brief glimpse of the landlord as he vanishes into the night. The smugglers pay him three times his normal daily rent. A three-room apartment with two beds and two sofas. Terrified, we fall asleep. By the time most of us wake, midday prayers are over and the sun is already past its height.

THE GROUP

The rhythms of life change. When you're a refugee, day becomes night and night day. Amar gets up and goes out to buy falafels for himself and the others. He quickly proves to be the one to take matters in hand, speaking and negotiating for the group. There are now thirteen of us in total; in the living room we flock to the plastic bags full of food. Everyone starts to talk about themselves. Brothers Alaa, thirty-one, and Hussan, twenty, talk about Damascus. Their family owns three carpet shops in the old town, but the war forced them to close. '90 per cent of our customers were foreigners.' Hussan would have been drafted into the military by now, so they both decided to flee. 'I'm doing this for my brother,' says Alaa. 'He wouldn't have survived the war.' Hussan still weighs 110 kilos, despite having had liposuction to remove another forty. Excess skin hangs off his stomach in pleats. Obesity is a big problem amongst the Syrian middle class. The two of them want to get to Italy and then continue on to Sweden, where their eldest brother arrived last year via the Mediterranean route. He was very lucky: his boat sank shortly before reaching Italy and he was already swimming when the Italian navy rescued him and the others. Their brother apparently raves about Sweden; he is doing a language course and wants to work in fast food.

Cousins Rabea and Asus come from a family of wealthy merchants. Rabea, who is twenty-two and – at 140 kilos – even fatter than Hussan, deserted from the Syrian military. He went into hiding for a few months with his grandparents in Damascus and later his relatives smuggled him over the border to Jordan with false papers. He tells us he had to pass thirteen checkpoints on his way out of Syria. He could have been executed on the spot at any one of them. 'I,' he declares solemnly over his food, 'have not been afraid of anything since.' He travels under a false name, calling himself Ahmed when around other people, and bribed his way to an Egyptian visa. He paid 2,400 dollars for it in Jordan. 'Do you want to see it?' he asks proudly, showing his forged passport with the bought visa. His passport makes its way around the room, from Alaa to Amar, from Amar to Hussan, from Hussan to me. Everyone admires the quality. 'It's better than my real one,' Amar says appreciatively. Rabea smiles proudly. When it comes to bribery and wheeling and dealing, he's the best in our group. He too wants to go to Sweden.

His cousin Asus, who worked as a bricklayer in Syria, is already engaged to a woman in Sweden. He sends her Viber messages every day from his smartphone. Asus is the group jester. He can make a joke out of any situation. He jokes about everything and everyone but can't stand jokes about himself. Asus is a very sensitive clown.

After they have eaten, they collapse into the chairs, flop onto the sofas, hunker down on the floor they have covered with cushions, and Asus recalls his five failed attempts to get to Europe. 'Five?' Amar asks in disbelief.

On his first attempt, Asus fled from northern Syria to Izmir in Turkey, where a rubber dinghy was to take him to the Greek islands. The anchor was still down when they were arrested by the coastguard. On his second attempt, he paid a smuggler who was going to take him over on a yacht; the coastguard arrived shortly before they were due to set off. The third time, the dinghy grazed a small reef after just one kilometre, tore open and sank. He survived by swimming to the coast. On his fourth try, the smugglers robbed them on the way to the beach and took off. The same thing happened on his fifth attempt.

This is his sixth go.

There's a call from Nuri, the agent, and the same as every time he rings, there's total silence. 'Tonight,' says Nuri. 'Get ready!' After a day of boredom, there's a sudden flurry of activity. We all pack our things and make ourselves seaworthy – whatever that means. Aside from Asus, none of our group has ever been to sea. Rabea, who professes to be a very poor swimmer, puts on a life jacket, a waterproof wrist pouch with a Velcro fastening for his phone, a balaclava and over that: sunglasses. Amar slips on the signal-blue jacket he hopes will protect against the wind and spray. They spend the most time hiding documents and money about their persons. The apartment is filled with the sound of tearing sticky tape as everyone wraps their essential documents in foil. The bedrooms, the kitchen, the toilet: the sound permeates every room. 'I heard they take all your bags away,' says Alaa. Everyone has their tricks, but Asus has the most absurd idea. He has sewn a cloth sausage down his underpants. 'They'll spot that immediately,' Alaa grouches. He too has fastened his money between his legs, but he reckons Asus is taking it a step too far. Asus gestures dismissively. He swaggers around the apartment with his legs spread and his hips thrust forwards.

Elias, the waiter from Hama, tapes his sister's medical reports to his stomach. He plans for her to follow later. Normally so irascible, he describes her as 'a gift from God.' His sister has Down's syndrome and asthma. 'I hope they'll be able to help her in Europe. These papers are more important than my money.'

Then we sit, jittery with nerves, and wait for several hours. Midnight has long since passed when Nuri calls to tell us the whole thing's off.

Three more days pass like this. Every attempt to get us on the boat fails. Today, Nuri tells us that the smugglers are having difficulty bribing the right coastguard officer. The next day, he says the waves are too high. The day after that, as he postpones the journey again, he tells us it's all in our best interests. 'Oh my God,' Amar sighs on the third evening, sitting in a circle with the others. He buries his face in his hands.

The shifts between boredom and extreme tension would be enough to wear down even the strongest amongst us. Alaa and Hussan catch colds and I am plagued by a persistent cough. Elias keeps us all awake at night talking on his phone. He is the last to get up, sleeping until early afternoon, and the last to go to bed in the early morning. The smugglers' apartment feels increasingly claustrophobic. Both balconies look out onto the dank alley, but if you turn your head all the way to the left, you can see the ocean. We watch wave after wave lapping the shore.

The smugglers have picked a good place to hide us. We are right in the centre of Alexandria, just behind the famous promenade where tens of thousands of tourists stroll, day and night, drawn to the sea. The refugees barely register in this chaotic mass of people. But at some point, Amar notices that the man on the main entrance is getting curious about the Syrians who come and go and are clearly neither workers nor tourists. 'Who are you?' he asks. In Egypt, you need to watch out for the doormen. They are at the heart of the secret service networks. 'He suspects something,' Amar warns the others hiding with us.

'Come back home!' Rolanda begs her husband on the phone. 'It's all just a huge nightmare.' Amar refuses. He would regret it for the rest of his life if he gave up now. 'Most people don't get a chance to pull themselves out of their shitty situation. But I can. At least I'm privileged enough to try.'

Amar phones Nuri and tries to convince him to hide us somewhere else. He tells him it's not safe here any more, and Nuri just laughs. He says we're too nervous. Nuri laughs, and Amar starts at every sound in the stairwell. More and more often, he or Alaa will jump up to listen at the door. If the doorman rings the police, the journey will be over before it's begun. Then, on the evening of the fourth day, our landlord storms in. 'Up, up!' he yells. This is the nervous landlord we saw just briefly on our first night. 'To the boat!' he yells. A minibus is waiting on the promenade. Alaa and Hussan grab their bags. Asus frantically wraps his papers in tape. Rabea urges him on, while Amar stands next to him wringing his hands. We have to go right now. 'Asus!' he says. 'Asus!'

Then we dash to the stairs, our bags on our backs, black woolly hats on our heads. We pass the doorman, who now knows exactly what we're doing here: trying to get on a boat. Our group hurries through the crowd of people strolling along the promenade, who turn to cast irritated glances our way. The waiting minibus is far too small to take everyone. A family – a mother and three children – has joined us. They say they want to get to Germany, to Munich. Asus lies across Rabea and Alaa. We stuff our bags between us, on our laps, under our chins; only our heads poke out at the top. We pray that the rucksacks and bags aren't visible from the outside.

The Toyota enters the city's broad and slow stream of traffic, affording us some safety. We are one of many minibuses. But soon we turn off into side streets, we go faster and faster, almost over-turning on corners, scraping several other vehicles. The driver is clearly on drugs, like almost all the people smugglers we encounter. Many get high on a mixture of the stimulant Tramadol, hashish and alcohol. 'He's going to kill us,' Alaa groans. After an hour, we come to a stop in an unlit industrial district. We pass an improvised checkpoint guarded by five men armed with hunting rifles. Two of them have dogs on ropes, and nervously patrol the alley.

'Please, tell me what's happening?' Amar's wife asks on the phone. She, her mother, her sister, two uncles and her elder daughters have gathered in her front room. She cannot cope with the tension on her own. 'I don't know,' Amar whispers, hidden behind his rucksack.

'Phones off!' calls one of the men, who bang on the outside of the windows. This alley is where the smugglers round up their passengers. Another minibus arrives and parks in front of ours by a factory wall. We see the outlines of other people behind the dark panes. 'Thirty-five adults and fifteen children,' Amar hears a man say as he walks past. Then nothing happens for several hours. We are packed in so tightly that we cut off the circulation in each other's legs. Wedged between items of luggage, I can only move my head a few millimetres. The smugglers tell us not to get out. But Elias still wants to climb out of the open window; he says he'll suffocate otherwise. Amar tries to hold him back, fearing our escorts' reaction. If they spotted him, it would be explosive, and Elias, impetuous as he is, would be unlikely to give in. But he ignores Amar, conceals himself behind the vehicle and, luckily, goes undiscovered.

The sun will soon be rising over the city, but Rabea – who is sitting further forward – hears that the smugglers are going to abort tonight's attempt. The waves are too strong. Shortly after, the driver of our minibus comes over and sits at the steering wheel. He doesn't talk to us or explain what is happening. The other bus starts up and disappears around the factory wall. 'I'm not driving,' our chauffeur yells. He starts to shout to one of the smugglers through the open side window. He wants more money. 'Fucker,' whispers Amar. The man standing by the window wipes his face almost obsessively. It's the drugs. The men shout at each other, the driver bangs his fist on the door, and then they agree on an extra ten Egyptian pounds. He drives off, again taking the corners at breakneck speed, zigzagging through the suburban neighbourhood.

A few streets later, we are overtaken by a green Kia that tries to stop us. Our driver curses and floors it, trying to lose them. For a while the two vehicles hurtle through the city side by side, then the Kia cuts us off on a bend. Two men pull our driver out of the bus. A stranger jams himself behind the wheel; he too says nothing. He puts the car in gear and we're off again, into darker and darker places, until he turns into a dead-end road where a group of men are waiting. They have broad shoulders and shaven necks, and grin as though there were something to celebrate.

'I think,' Amar whispers, 'we've just been kidnapped. God be with us.'

KIDNAPPED

Alexandria has two parallel worlds. In the daytime, people wear uniforms – sometimes plain clothes – and while they are often corrupt, the identification they carry gives them legitimacy. The police. The other world is the *baltagiya*, which takes over once night closes in. The *baltagiya* is made up of the small criminal gangs that extort protection money, deal drugs and run prostitution rings. The *baltagiya* is like a criminal bazaar where money can buy you anything. We, the refugees who want to leave the country, are a commodity for the Alexandrian mafia to trade as they wish.

Stanislav and I are in a particularly risky spot. What will our abductors do if they discover who we really are?

One of the men approaches the bus and wrenches open the slid-ing door. 'Call your agents!' Rabea phones Mohamed, the foppish dealer who took him to the meeting point in Cairo, and gets him to speak with the man. Soon another minibus parks behind us. It's full of young Egyptians – the crew of the vessel that was supposed to take us from the beach to the fishing boat. They appear to have been kidnapped as well. 'We have to rush them,' says hot-headed Elias. 'All together, as one! Then we'll have a chance!' 'Elias's right,' says Amar. 'We can't afford to be cowards. We'll simply knock them down!' But we'll have to leave our bags. 'Forget your bags,' he says. He can't see any weapons on the men around our minibus, but thinks at the very least they'll have knives under their shirts. One of our abductors walks up and down outside, frantically making phone calls. A short time later he gets back behind the wheel and starts the engine. 'We're sorting out the problem,' he says. 'Don't be afraid.'

Again we travel into the unknown, entering ever poorer areas. We see visitors streaming out of the mosques from morning prayers. Our abductor stops in the courtyard of a residential complex with rundown seven-storey blocks, surrounded by rubbish and puddles of dirty water. 'You are free,' he tells us, but it's a lie. We are to spend the day in an apartment here. 'What's the problem?' asks Amar. Their gang has had a dispute with the leader of the gang that's supposed to get us to Europe. Our abductor says that the boss of our group has betrayed his boss. He explains that the gangs divided the coast into several zones. They allow the others to use their particular zones as long as payment is made. Our group's smugglers didn't stick to the rules last time. 'That's just chaos,' Amar complains. 'Such a sensitive business needs to be organised perfectly!' Our abductor laughs.

As night begins to fade we hurry into a stairwell, led by a drunken man into an apartment without water. It's clearly being renovated. He talks gibberish and tries to blackmail us for 1,500 dollars. Amar struggles to understand him. The man becomes abusive; he has a flick knife on his waistband. Amar embraces him, kisses him and thanks him for his patience, telling him that, unfortunately, we can't give him any money. Furious, the man warns us not to make a sound or look out of the windows. 'You have no idea what's going on around you,' the drunk man says before closing the door behind us.

'Hello?!' Hussan calls after him through the intercom. 'My friend, why have you shut us in?'

These men, who wanted to finally be free, have never been less free than now. Around fifty-five square metres are all that remain. Two rooms with three beds, a filthy kitchen and a toilet without water. In a built-in wardrobe, Amar finds luggage from refugees held here before us, clothes for women and children. 'I wonder what became of them?'

For the first hour of captivity, most of our group remain standing; they refuse to bow to the pressure of our new situation, to lie on the dusty beds. They are perplexed, still wearing the jackets they donned for the crossing. Gradually they begin to accept their plight, taking off their clothes layer by layer, lying on the mattresses, the dusty tiles, completely exhausted. And then they fall asleep.

Only Alaa and I stay awake; he doesn't trust the silence, and I am still too pumped up. Alaa is lying on the bed next to his sleeping brother when we hear someone trying to open the door, scratching and scraping at the lock. I decide it would be wiser to keep to my mattress; I'm still afraid that our abductors will discover our true identities. Alaa looks around the apartment for a weapon, a stick, a knife, but comes up empty-handed. Suddenly, the door opens gently. Three men – including the one who brought us here – appear in the doorway and walk in. 'How can I help you?' asks Alaa. They wanted to bring us some coffee, the trio say. They even have a tray of coffee cups. 'It's the wrong time of night to be drinking coffee,' says Alaa. He takes the tray and they leave. We will never know what the intruders actually wanted. To see if we were awake? To snatch our bags? The night-time visit remains a mystery.

On our third day of confinement, Alaa asks Amar if he can have one of his Xanax tablets. He still can't sleep. With space so restricted, tensions are rising between Alaa and his brother Hussan, whom he accuses of being lazy and never making decisions for himself. 'At home in Damascus, he just played on his Game Boy and messed around on Facebook,' he complains to Amar when Hussan leaves the room for a moment. Hussan got to 150 kilos before he went under the knife. The whole family nags Hussan to change. Alaa gets upset by Hussan's apathy, and Hussan gets upset that Alaa is upset. Hussan feels patronised by Alaa; he's twenty years old, not a child to be disciplined. The pair exchange wounded glances.

'Am I a bad brother?' asks Alaa.

At least our abductors send us food and water. We ignore their order to keep the windows closed; we'd suffocate otherwise. Hussan and Rabea, who each smoke two packs of cigarettes a day, lean against the window ledge and look down into the courtyard. The family trying to get to Munich are in one of the apartments opposite. We often see the children sunning themselves on the balcony. Nuri, the agent in Cairo, consoles us on the phone. He says they are all working on a solution. He gets our hopes up every afternoon, only to dash them again by late evening. 'If you can't get us to Italy,' Amar yells, 'then at least get us out of this shithole!'

Every night, Alaa and Hussan go hunting for midges, smacking the walls, doors and cupboards with hand towels, lunging around the apartment until early morning. The walls of our prison ring with their blows.

Time loses all meaning. Hours, days, pass as we doze. Car horns blare below. We hear barking dogs, the singsong of scrap-metal dealers dragging their wares through the streets. A merciless void. We stare at the white walls, at crazy-making shadows cast by the sun.

'When I get to Sweden I swear I'll change,' says Hussan, who shares my blanket at night. 'I'll be a better person in Sweden. I'll stop smoking. I'll exercise. Sweden will give me a second chance.' He knows we've never been so far from Sweden.

And then the chance to escape almost goes very wrong. Amar is never off the phone, threatening that we'll simply leave through this flimsy door, the whole lot of us, if the gangs can't come to some arrangement. It clearly has an effect. On the fourth day, around noon, agent Mohamed announces that a white minibus will be coming to pick us up. One of the abductors has given us the key to the door. When the white bus drives up, we scurry down the stairs one by one, rucksacks on our backs and black woolly hats on our heads, hoping the neighbours don't see us. We hear voices from an open door on the second floor, then we squeeze into the bus waiting outside with its door open. It's the wrong one. 'Who are you?' asks the driver, turning in his seat to look at us. He's here to take a group of Egyptian day-workers to their construction site. He sees the fear in our eyes.

Panicked, we murmur our apologies. 'Our mistake,' Amar tells the driver as we squeeze our way out again. Previously invisible, we have inadvertently made ourselves conspicuous. We hurry back up the dark stairs and past the open door that is now completely silent, no more voices, as though someone has heard us. One after another we dart through the crack of light. One floor above, we wait outside our apartment, Rabea's eyes wide, Hussan's breathing laboured, until, last of all, Amar makes it up and unlocks the door to our old prison. We lock the door behind us and listen anxiously. No sound from the stairwell.

Finally, another white minibus arrives. Ours. 'I'm very tired,' says Amar.

Our abductors, men in their thirties, pick us up and chauffeur us to freedom. They apologise, try to be friendly, tell us not to take it personally. They declare their love for Syrians; they hate Egypt, we're right to leave. 'Egypt is rotting,' one of them says. After driving a few kilometres, he slides open the door and we find ourselves back on Alexandria's promenade after four days of imprisonment. A smiling Mohamed greets us in his white suit and peaked cap. We've never been happier to see him.

'Welcome back!' he says, flinging open his arms and giving us his best salesman's smile. He takes us to one of the apartment blocks on the promenade, fifteenth floor, three balconies. We step out onto the balconies, high above the sea. So much light after so much darkness. Mohamed tells us later that the smugglers paid our kidnappers a ransom of 35,000 Egyptian pounds.

THE SEA I

We have our lives back. Although suddenly free to make decisions, we know how fleeting this moment will be. What should we do? Give up? This journey has been a nightmare, and it hasn't even begun. We spend the whole evening on one of the balconies in our new apartment. The view of the Mediterranean is spectacular.

Impulsive as ever, Elias decides to leave us. He wants to switch to a different smuggling gang. He doesn't think ours will manage it; they have problems with the coastguard and with other gangs too. He calls a rival group's sales agent. 'Come to us,' the agent says. 'We have a boat leaving tonight.' Elias takes his small rucksack and decides to go. Alaa and Amar beg him to stay. We're a group, they plead. Each new person who joins us brings uncertainty, suspicion. Every person who leaves makes us less safe. Elias is undecided; he sets his bag down. The others talk him around. He doesn't know what to do, he keeps picking up his rucksack and putting it down again. He goes out the door and returns a few minutes later. Like a wild animal backed into a corner. This continues for a while; he'll go out and then come back, out and back, until he leaves, for good.

Alaa wants to carry on; he'll suffocate in Egypt. He'll always be a second-class citizen here. His brother hesitates. He doesn't know whether his nerves can take it. 'I'll do whatever Alaa does,' he says finally. 'No!' Alaa shouts, staring at his brother. It's time for Hussan to make his own decisions; he won't take responsibility for him any longer. 'You need to figure out what you want!' Hussan says nothing. Amar also wants to carry on. 'I don't want to have any regrets. If something happens to one of my daughters here, I'll never forgive myself.'

Rabea nods towards the sea. 'We have to press on. The worst is behind us.' In the middle of the night, Hussan lets out a long sigh and repeats what he has resolved. 'When I get to Sweden, I'll change. I'll study. And work. I need to get away from here, I need to get on the boat.'

Then we spend hours staring out at the dark ocean, hundreds of lights dancing on its surface. The fishing fleet, as beautiful as stardust. One of these lights is the boat that has been sailing up and down the coast for days, waiting for us. As morning approaches, the lights start to go out. Before long the ocean lies naked and grey before the city, making no promises.

Amar stares into the distance until the last light is extinguished, and then goes to bed.

During this time, thousands of refugees are sailing to Sicily, 1,500 kilometres away, making the most of the first weeks of favourable weather. The sea is at its most gentle in spring and autumn. Over the winter months more and more refugees have gathered on the North African coast; now that spring is here they will attempt the crossing. They say there are 600,000 people on the southern Mediterranean coastline, waiting for the right moment. But the EU's interior ministers are piling on the pressure; they want Libya and Egypt to stop the boats. They give and withdraw money, rewarding and punishing. The Egyptian military junta, attempting to crush the burgeoning democracy, sees an opportunity to present itself to Europe as a reliable force for order. They hunt refugees, tighten coastal controls and send hundreds to detention camps every week.

While Europe puts on a charitable show when refugees manage to reach the Mediterranean's north coast, on the sea's south coast Europe wages a relentless proxy war.

The boat we are due to board is twenty-four metres long and can take around 300 refugees. We hear this from the head of the smuggling ring, who introduces himself as Abu Hassan. He owns the boat, or so he claims. He has come to our hiding place to restore our trust. A small man with a pointed beard, he immediately puts his feet up on the table. 'This journey is as important for me as it is for you,' he says. He's worried we might change our minds and use a different smuggling group. 'I've spent a lot of money on you already.' The ransom, the minibuses, renting a succession of apartments. A week ago he sent 1,000 loaves of bread to the boat; they're probably mouldy by now.

Abu Hassan explains that four major people smugglers divided up the Egyptian market between them. He is one of them; the others are the 'Doctor', the 'Hanafi' and Abu Ahmed. Their refugee business flourished last year; he alone sent thirty-five boats to Italy. Our journey will open the current season. Your outcome, says Abu Hassan, will determine how the whole season goes.

He promises the coastguard will let us pass. 'They are my people.' He is paying the officer and his men 30,000 euros. The officer gets half and the rest is divided between his underlings. The coastguard usually demands a flat fee of 100 euros per passenger. They don't receive the money until the vessel has made it into international waters. But at the moment, the smugglers are proving to be their own worst enemies. 'It's ruining the whole market.' Everyone wants a bigger slice of this lucrative pie. Abu Hassan explains how they sabotage each other, telling the police about each other's plans. Two days ago, the captain of a ship with a full load of refugees returned to the harbour and handed all the passengers over to the coastguard; he'd been paid to do so by rival smugglers. One person's loss is another's profit. They damage their competitors' reputations to boost their own. But it's gone too far now. The big four are meeting in Alexandria to make peace.

'Can we take our bags?' Rabea asks as the head smuggler leaves. 'You all have so much luggage,' Abu Hassan answers evasively. 'You wouldn't take that much on a plane.' Alaa wants to know how long the crossing will last. 'Six days,' says Abu Hassan. 'Nothing at all for a trip to paradise.'

In the ensuing days we switch apartments three more times. Twice we move within the same building; the landlords are worried about trouble with the police. Then the smugglers take us to the opposite end of the promenade and set us up on the twelfth floor of a different block. We may have lost our sea view, but we have a bath and hot water.

Changing location is always risky. Enemy gangs are supposedly lying in wait, hoping for another chance to kidnap us. Informers for other mafia clans are spotted on the opposite side of the street, in front of our building, gaunt young men who loiter, feigning disinterest, cigarettes between their fingers, waiting.

We reporters have a new problem, the greatest of our journey so far: Ismail, a stout and pockmarked man who represents Abu Hassan, the smuggling king. All of a sudden he stands before us, hand extended, and greets us in Russian. According to our cover story, Stanislav and I are from a republic in the Caucasus. Stanislav speaks fluent Russian, but I don't. Stanislav comes to my rescue, talking to the smuggler in Russian, telling him all about our plight. I signal that I have a cold and am depressed and tired. I withdraw and pretend to sleep. Sometimes for a few minutes, sometimes for a whole day. My lack of Russian remains a secret.

Elias, who upped and left, calls to report that his new smugglers also lied. They haven't managed to get round the coastguard either. Like us, Elias is hiding in Alexandria, just a few streets away.

To make matters worse, the weather has turned against us too. A strong wind from the west batters our balcony door. Amar closes it and uses a rag as a draught excluder. We lie on the carpets and sofas under thick blankets. An area of low pressure just off Europe. Even without elaborate explanations from our smugglers, we know there's no point in trying to sail.

'I feel like a donkey,' complains Rabea. 'Just sleeping, eating, shitting and sleeping all day.'

The wind picks up even more as evening approaches, whistling sharply through the window frames. We are gathered around the television watching *X-Men*, a fantasy film about mutants trying to live amongst humans undetected, when there's a knock at the door.

Amar and Alaa jump up from the sofas and I hide in the bedroom, covering myself with a blanket in case it's Ismail again, the smuggler who speaks Russian. Rabea goes to the door and hesitates. Although people often knock on the door, it scares us each time. It could be the police. Or rival smugglers who've tracked us down and come to abduct us. Rabea unlocks the door and opens it just a crack, ready to shut it again if necessary.

It's Mohamed in his peaked cap. He's brought two new people, a carpenter and a sculptor, to hide with us. We know them already.

They were quartered with the family trying to get to Munich. They both come from southern Syria, like the mother and her daughters. The smuggler whispers to Amar; the carpenter was harassing one of the daughters, secretly watching her in the bathroom. 'We need to separate them from the family. Keep an eye on them.'

Our two new companions keep to themselves. The sculptor is hunchbacked and wears a denim cap decorated with an eagle; the stocky carpenter has a walrus moustache and wears a muscle shirt. They make their own tea, whisper to each other as we whisper amongst ourselves. They avoid us and most of us avoid them, particularly Alaa. He watches them suspiciously. He won't sit next to them, stares at them from a distance.

'Those are not good people,' he murmurs.

But then, a good week after we left Cairo with Amar, the moment finally comes. The minibuses pick us up, we travel out of Alexandria, and run to the sea as fast as we can.

THE BEACH II

'Run, you sons of bitches!' shouts the boy, still too young for facial hair, whacking us with his stick. 'Run!'

The beach is flat and sandy. When we finally reach it, we are ordered to lie on the ground. We are divided into three lots of twenty refugees, a few metres between each group. Hussan is so inflexible that he can't kneel down fast enough. His brother grabs his jacket and pulls him to the ground.

The beach is the most dangerous part of our passage to Europe. The beach attracts scavengers. The beach is where predators converge from land and sea. We are now at our most vulnerable. Bandits will often attack, beat and rob refugees on the beach. Sometimes it is the smugglers, themselves unsatisfied with their commissions, who rob their passengers. The coastguard could turn up at any time, by water or land, with dogs. Enormous factories bathe the area in light. Abu Qir Bay is one of Egypt's largest industrial harbours. Behind us, on the mainland, an infernal display of red, orange and yellow. Before us, freight ships at anchor illuminate the ocean with their signal lights. Smoke drifts above our heads in lurid colours.

'You father to the fatherless,' Alaa calls out to the water, overcome by the moment.

Amar speaks to his wife. 'We're by the sea,' he says as he lies on the sand. 'I don't know how much longer I'll be able to call. If you don't hear anything else, we've made it.' Two motorboats come racing towards us.

The young men are the first to run, grasping for the hull of the front boat, trying to pull themselves up, falling off and trying again. Amar hangs back as though paralysed. He's afraid of crowds and wants to get on last, but the last ones often get left behind on the beach. Luckily, the second crew spot us. We have to wade in up to our chests to reach the boat. I give overweight Rabea a helping hand from below him, whilst someone else pulls him up, then a hand reaches down to me. I seize it and it drags me up and across the deck where Amar lies breathless. Bissan, the diabetic girl, crouches next to us. She looks to the shore and cries and screams. Her voice grows louder und even drowns out the motor.

Her mother stands in the waves in her black hijab and holds up her arms. She calls after the boat, which is already turning out to sea. The rucksack with the insulin floats in the water; a wave tore it from Bissan's hands. Families often become separated when getting on the boats. Again and again, children arrive in Italy without their parents. Once you're on the boat, there's no going back. The sculptor who came to live with us promised he would carry Bissan through the surf. Because he lived with the family for weeks. Because he is one of the few with a life jacket. Instead, he dumped her in the water. He risked her life to secure himself a place on the first boat. The crew of the second boat pulled her on board but forgot her mother.

The girl's cries are so loud that the men turn back, cursing, pull her mother on board and fish the insulin out of the water with a stick. Her rucksack, her lifeline, is shoved into her hands.

Then we head out to sea, spray washing over us. We hear the keel slapping the water and the girl's unrelenting cries, completely distraught. The smugglers yell at her whilst her mother and sister try to reassure her. Amar slides over to Bissan and asks, 'Are you scared?' 'No,' she says, gradually growing calmer. 'I can't be. If I get scared, the sugar shock will kill me.'

The coast narrows to a thin line on the horizon. With just nine of us – the others all threw themselves into the first vessel – the boat is not quite full. One crew member keeps watch on the prow whilst another sits by the motor. The boss stands next to him at the rudder, holding course for the open sea, but soon he's swearing into his phone. 'Where's that son of a bitch now?!' he shouts to the others. He tries to contact the captain of the main ship without success. 'He said he'd be in position in fifteen minutes!' Suddenly the outboard motor starts to splutter. It wheezes, spits water and dies. There's complete silence all around us.

The refugees look at the crew. The men drop anchor and try to get the motor going again, yanking the starter cable, yanking it again and again. The boss opens the motor hatch whilst another calls the captain of the first boat, which sailed parallel to us for quite some time before overtaking us and disappearing into the darkness. He tells the captain to drop off his passengers and turn back to retrieve us.

Then the motor springs to life.

Again the boat races over the crests of the waves. The lookout at the prow says he can see the ship. In under five minutes we will be in international waters and the Egyptian coastguard won't be able to touch us. One of the smugglers moves around the boat telling us to hand over any Egyptian pounds. 'You won't be needing them any more.'

'That's it!' he says shortly after, pointing to the many lights on the ocean. Somewhere out there is the ship. Amar lies on his back and looks up at the sky, his hands behind his head and a gentle smile on his face. He took a double dose of Xanax before we set off. Rabea laughs, punches the air, claps Amar on the leg, beaming. For the first time, we think we've made it. Stanislav and I feel the same; by now our feelings are practically indistinguishable from those of the refugees. Italy is within our grasp, Sweden, Germany, a new life, dreams, months of preparation – and then the boat heads to an island and the smugglers push us overboard.

One after another we fall into the water.

'I don't know what's happening, Rolanda,' Amar tells his wife on the phone a little while later. Luckily his phone didn't get wet. 'We're on an island. The boats are gone. I don't know what they're planning.'

The first boat's passengers have also been left here, and we are reunited with Alaa, Hussan and Asus. The crew told them that the boats would be back for us soon. We form groups and settle on the crest of a hill. Most of us shiver with cold, soaked through and exposed to the wind. Alaa unpacks some large plastic bags and lies on the shrubbery that covers the island. He pulls a bag over his legs and stomach and up to his chest. Amar copies him and pulls his hood over his face until only his mouth remains visible. He bombards Abu Hassan with one phone call after another. The smuggling king promises to send new boats.

This, we find out later, is Nelson Island. A small island measuring 100 x 300 metres, this was where Admiral Nelson defeated Napoleon's fleet in 1798. As the full moon emerges from behind the clouds, the dunes are bathed in an eerie silver light. The island almost seems like some kind of limbo, neither earthly nor heavenly, detached from everything. As I walk, I half expect the ground to shatter like glass.

The smugglers return, this time with a somewhat larger boat. The passengers dash towards it, running through the water without much regard for each other. They push off from the muddy bottom, jumping up to hang off the railings, all together, all on the same side until the boat threatens to capsize in the surf. The crew defend themselves with sticks, beating the desperate refugees to stop themselves from going under. Amar, Stanislav and I stay on the beach with Bissan and her family. Amar's fear of crowds has returned. The boat speeds out to sea, heavily laden, but turns back immediately. Standing on the beach, it takes us a while to figure out what's wrong.

Then we see two coastguard speedboats behind the smugglers. Two shadows with red flashing lights. The smugglers throw the refugees into the surf, kicking them, hitting them, bags landing in the water. We run away from the sea and further into the island, in a futile attempt to hide.

'It's over, isn't it?' Amar whispers to me in the deep trench where we and four others are hiding.

Group by group, the soldiers force us to come out. Refugees have often been shot during their arrest. Some hide behind rocks in the surf until they get cold and give up. Bissan's family press themselves into a hollow. Others only have time to flatten themselves against the ground. The soldiers comb the island with searchlights. They close in on our hiding place and shout to us to come out.

Amar and I climb out of the trench, our hands up, dazzled by the light. We approach them slowly and suddenly they fire two, three warning shots from automatic rifles with live ammunition. We fall to our knees as they yell commands I don't understand. Amar, who usually translates for us, is petrified. They force us into a row, our heads lowered in an attitude of submission. Our identification papers, if we have any, must be placed on our heads. Some people get a kick in the back.

So ends tonight's dream.

'Did you think you were in Sicily already?' laughs the officer on the command vessel taking us back to the harbour. He is pleased with himself. He'll be getting a bonus or commendation for this.

PRISON I

Those who failed are imprisoned in an empty room measuring thirty-five square metres, a barred window revealing nothing but mounds of rubbish. We have to enter in two lines. It's been a day and a half since we last slept. 'Kneel down!' roars the officer on duty. 'I'm going to prepare you for the darkest hour of your lives! Listen to what I say.' Then we are led into the communal cell. We are now in the custody of the National Security Police, a sort of Egyptian FBI, which at this time is also staging political show trials for the military junta. No one tells us the charges, no one explains the procedure. They simply lock us in this room. We lie down on the bare concrete floor because there are no beds and pull our last dry clothes over our bodies because there are no blankets. We have to wait until later that night for the friends we called to bring us wool blankets and food.

At this time, detention camps for arrested Syrian refugees are popping up in the larger towns and cities along the coast. Ours appears to be one of the better ones. Other camps are holding more than 200 people without food or clean water.

We start off with thirty-eight people, but soon more than sixty of us are jostling for space. The room gets noticeably warmer with each new group. We sleep shoulder to shoulder. It's a gathering of Syria's middle class. The owner of a textiles factory from Daraa with his wife and their two young sons, a chocolate-factory owner from Darayya and his two daughters, a cameraman who used to work for Syrian television, several engineers and teachers. Some families were torn apart on the beach; some made it onto the first boat, others were arrested on the beach. Some got as far as the main ship but there wasn't enough food and it had to turn back. They recall how they and their children were set down on a sandbank, terrified of being overwhelmed by the tide. How fishermen took them from the island – after being paid – and then handed them over to the police.

The youngest detainee is five years old, imprisoned with her two sisters.

Every evening the prison is filled with terrible wails. We hear the screams of people being beaten and the shouts of the perpetrators. In January 2011, when Hosni Mubarak's dictatorship began to falter, this prison was one of the first buildings in Alexandria to be stormed. Massive crowds overpowered the guards, freed the prisoners, looted the prison and set it alight. Even then, it was known as one of Alexandria's worst torture chambers. After just a brief hiatus, the torturers have returned. Troops of painters work frantically on various levels of the prison, redecorating the walls, painting over the fire damage, soot and burn marks. They paint the walls calmly as people scream all around them. 'If you grow up in Egypt,' one of our guards tells me, 'you learn to block out these screams.'

Amar has saved us a few square metres below the only window. Even in the cell our group stays together. Hussan is silent, hardly ever speaking and sleeping a lot, all the time in fact. Alaa rarely speaks to his younger brother. 'I didn't realise he was so unfit.' He even had to carry Hussan's rucksack when they sprinted to the boat. 'I shouldn't have brought him along,' says Alaa. He complains that Hussan can't run or swim, that he's mentally weak. 'My brother has never experienced real life.' In Damascus he helped out in the family shops but he never really had to work. Alaa and the staff always looked after things. Hussan was mainly into his Game Boy.

The two brothers lie next to each other, and are delighted to speak to anyone, except each other. After a few days, when Hussan has almost stopped speaking altogether and only broods and stares vacantly, Alaa caves in. 'Brother,' he asks, 'you're not falling ill, are you?'

A bureaucrat in a brown suit will judge our cases. One after another we are taken off to be questioned. He doesn't introduce himself, puts on a theatrical voice. Questioning is a ritual of submission. Amar is in the interrogation room for two hours. When he finally emerges, something has changed. This clever man of action – the heart of his family, a man who managed to stay good-humoured and optimistic when first imprisoned – is falling apart before our eyes. He sits listlessly, his eyes closed, his face blank.

Upon being arrested, we reporters had to reveal our true identities. Like all the others, we are charged with leaving the country illegally. The German and Czech embassies intervene on our behalf; Stanislav is from the Czech Republic. After nine days we are deported to Turkey.

PART TWO

FAREWELL II

The sea is a black mass beyond the window of seat 8A. The Turkish Airlines plane left Alexandria just before midnight. My deportation flight.

Stanislav Krupař and I have been spared the indignity of handcuffs. Police officers took us from our cell in the prison to a cell in the airport. A delicate boy from Bangladesh, also awaiting deportation, lay on some cardboard on the floor. He was shaking all over, suffering from an infection of some description. We received our papers at the departure gate. In a matter of seconds, those papers transformed us into different people. From prisoners to privileged frequent flyers. To residents of that Elysium known as Europe. Previously confined to just a few square metres, now the world is our oyster. I hold my maroon passport with 'European Union' embossed on the cover in gold.

Muted lights guide us into an aircraft playing upbeat music. The air is scented. We are greeted by the laughter of elegant attendants. 'Would you like tea or coffee?' All the structures that previously prevented us from crossing borders are now on our side, enticing us with adverts and low, low prices. Everything that held us back is now working to get us to our destination as quickly as possible. After take-off, I rest my cheek against the window. I'm exhausted. For a long time I stare at the sea, at all the tiny lights below me, which are fishing boats. One of them might be the ship we tried, and failed, to reach. The Mediterranean, that for so many is an insurmountable obstacle, that for so many means death, we cross effortlessly and half asleep. On this particular night, it feels truly obscene.

We return to our homes – Stanislav to Prague, I to Reutlingen in southern Germany – but we keep in touch with our fellow refugees.

For Amar, Alaa and Hussan, the real nightmare is yet to come.

Over the next few weeks, the Middle Eastern crisis – the thing driving people across the sea to Europe – gets worse. Old wars become bloodier and new wars ignite.

THE WARS

Assad's war: the regime has been driven out of large sections of the country, severely weakened but far from beaten. Most of Assad's support comes from Alawites no longer only fearing the loss of power, but of their very existence. There have been so many massacres. This war has the potential for genocide, on both sides. There is no chance of reconciling the Sunnis, who make up most of the rebel forces, and the Shiite Alawites.

The Sunnis threaten to push the Alawites to the Mediterranean. If the rebels achieve a major breakthrough on a particular front, the Alawite population flees in panic. Conversely, many Sunnis have now left their villages. Most of the refugees are Sunnis. Assad's air force, predominantly Alawite, systematically bombs Sunni towns and villages to ruins. And by the fourth year of the war, the rebels too are exhausted. Most of the people who began the uprising in early 2011 – first with peaceful protests, then with armed attacks – have fled, been injured or died. On some sections of the Syrian frontline, combat units sustain losses of 75 per cent in just a few months.

Gang wars: when rebels are killed, they are replaced by people with very little connection to the values of the resistance. Dozens of larger rebel groups fight the regime, but increasingly fight amongst themselves too. There are hundreds of militias with shifting allegiances, some of them kidnappers and bandits who terrorise villages that, in turn, defend themselves with their own militia.

The war against extremists: the more moderate rebels of the Free Syrian Army and Islamic Front fight against the radical group Islamic State (IS). These conflicts are said to have claimed 6,000 lives already.

The civil war between the radicalised: the Islamists fight each other too. The al-Nusra militia, which belongs to the global al-Qaeda terrorist network, fights IS, which was officially expelled from al-Qaeda. It was too extreme even for Bin Laden's successors.

The Kurdish war: everyone against the Kurds, and the Kurds against everyone. In northern Syria, the Peshmerga wage a fierce defence against radical and liberal rebels who regularly invade Kurdish settlements. They believe that the Kurds support the regime and dispute their claims to be true Muslims.

The coming Iraq war: in June 2014, most of Iraq's Sunni population rises up against the government in Baghdad. Supporters of the old regime under Saddam Hussein join with IS troops. Within days, they have occupied large parts of central Iraq and the government army threatens to collapse. The IS militia executes thousands of soldiers in mass shootings. They drive Christians out of Mosul and set fire to churches. The Shiites also call their militias to arms in the hope of defending at least their core areas and the capital, Baghdad. Iraq is on the brink of collapse.

All of these wars are a succession of offensives and counter-offensives. Villages burn and fields are torched. After each new offensive, more families decide to flee, to the next village, across the next border, to the next coast, across the sea.

THE BEACH III

At a later date, Alaa and Hussan, the brothers from Syria, recall how they left through the main entrance of an Alexandria prison after three weeks of captivity. The group of refugees finally disbands. They leave Amar behind; he won't be released for quite a few days yet. As a farewell gift, he gives them the three life jackets I bought for us from a canoe shop in Germany's Swabian region and the water purification tablets.

They embrace in front of the building that held them for so long. 'Hey,' someone calls to them. 'There's a new boat leaving tonight. Come with us!' 'No,' says Alaa, 'we're going to Cairo. We need to rest for a while.' He asks himself how anyone can start calling smugglers whilst still outside the prison. On the way to the train station, Alaa's hips start to hurt; he hasn't moved properly for ages.

Their brother Mohamed meets them at Cairo station. He runs a shop and has an apartment with a hot shower. Alaa stands underneath it for what feels like an eternity.

On the first night, he wakes up, terrified, asking himself, 'Where am I? In the cell? With the smugglers?'

Less than two days after their release, they get a call from Bashar, the friend who was travelling with them. What's your plan? Are we going to try again? Alaa prefers to wait a while and see whether any boats actually make it to Europe. But, actually, he's already made his decision. He orders a new credit card; he lost the old one on the journey. Then Bashar rings again. The landlord of the last apartment in Alexandria – where we hid before being arrested – claims that a good ship with reliable people will be leaving soon. It costs 2,400 dollars.

The brothers have learned from their first failed crossing. Alaa has the number of a prison officer who promised to help him (for 100 euros) should he be arrested again. He will release them before they can be registered by the prison bureaucrats. This time, Alaa and Hussan take their orange life jackets and a large supply of dates, pitted to reduce the weight. They also pack fewer clothes to keep their rucksacks as light as possible.

Alaa proceeds with mixed feelings; he's never been one to let himself be carried away by his emotions. He goes because he has to. His life is still in Damascus. Alaa grew up amongst arcades with ancient Roman and Ottoman columns, a child of the bazaar, this picture-book Oriental world so fascinating to European tourists. The family shop sits like a cave in the ancient vaulted walls. In his world there is no sun, just gold and gleaming fabrics. He loves the chaos of buying and selling, with rules for nothing and yet for everything. 'I can spend half a day there, meeting friends, drinking tea, without spending a single cent.'

Their brother Mohamed takes them to the station, waving to them until the train starts moving at around nine. As always, Bashar is late. 'Bashar's pretty easy-going,' says Alaa. He's completely different, uneasy, constantly on guard, wanting to have everything under control. The train is already trundling out of the station when they see Bashar: he's running down the platform with his long black hair and his little rucksack. He manages to reach the carriage door, holds on to the handle, jumps up and is soon sitting down next to them. 'You really are unbelievable,' Alaa tells Bashar.

On the day that Alaa and Hussan attempt their second crossing, Amar is released from prison in Alexandria. He's at the end of his tether, tired, drained. His wife wants to visit him in prison, to see him one more time before he's deported, but Amar refuses. 'Amar, it'll be a very long time before we can hold each other again,' his wife pleads. 'I don't want you to see me like this,' says Amar. Shortly before his deportation, he speaks to his youngest daughter, who is five. 'Papa, when are you going to come home and bring me some chocolate?' The police lock him in the same airport cell that housed me and Stanislav one month before. He is booked on the same flight to Istanbul on which we were deported. In a last show of mercy, the Egyptian authorities don't deport refugees back to Syria. They give him a choice: Lebanon or Turkey.

'I was flying into a void,' he tells me later. 'Until then I had always known what would happen next. But not now.' Rabea, the fattest one in our group, who fled Syria as a deserter, waits for him in Turkey beyond the passport desks. He was deported a few days earlier. 'Welcome!' Rabea grins. They take the tram to the area where Rabea has rented an apartment with five other Syrian refugees. 'Rabea, I can't live here with all of you,' says Amar. After so many weeks in prison, he needs some privacy. Rabea takes him to a cheap hotel on the same street, fifty dollars a night, breakfast included. It may be early afternoon, but Amar can't stay awake much longer. After a quick call to his wife, he falls asleep – and hopes to never wake up.

In Alexandria, Alaa, Hussan and Bashar go to the apartment block at the east end of the promenade. They take the lift to the twelfth floor, with Koran suras playing as muzak in the background, and meet the landlord in the apartment we previously shared. The land-lord is called Abu Ibrahim, a softly spoken and tall man, a Syrian Palestinian who has lived in Egypt for a long time. 'Something must have gone wrong last time,' he says by way of greeting.

He tells them that in the lead-up to the Egyptian elections, the military wanted to show its strength. For their campaign to succeed, they had to style themselves as an alternative to the sup-posed chaos of the Democrats and Muslim Brotherhood. And so they made it difficult for boats to get to Europe. But now that the elections are over, and the army's commander-in-chief has been elected president, the situation is completely different. 'Trust me,' he says. 'I'll get you on the ship with the best smugglers.' Previously satisfied with renting his apartment to smugglers, Abu Ibrahim has discovered that he could earn a lot more from the refugees. He wants to become an agent. Low outlay and risk, high profits. He gets to keep 300 dollars per customer. Three weeks ago he put Asus, the joker of our group, onto a boat. The journey took five days and now he's in Sweden.

But there's just one catch.

Abu Ibrahim insists on payment up front. When Alaa still thought I was a refugee, he told me never to trust anyone who insists on payment up front. You'll never get to Europe that way. Abu Ibra-him also wanted Asus to put up a guarantee. Asus gave the money to a friend and asked him to move into Abu Ibrahim's apartment until Asus arrived in Italy. When Asus called from Italy, his friend handed over the money and left. 'Let's do the same,' advises Bashar.

'There's no one I can ask,' Alaa claims evasively. Unlike Bashar, he understands the full implications. Abu Ibrahim is demanding collateral, a hostage.

Other agents try to poach them. Nuri, Amar's friend who brokered our last journey, calls them often. Touting safe passage the following day, cheaper than last time, they get a discount for spending time in prison. 'Come to me, friends,' he says. Alaa, Hussan and Bashar go to bed nervous, afraid. Last time they at least made it out to sea; now they're failing on land. They spend the night pondering whether to return to Cairo or to give up altogether and abandon their dream, just like any unobtainable dream. The alternative is madness.

'Hussan?' Alaa asks in the night. 'Give up – now?'

The next morning Ibrahim is friendly again. Surprisingly solici-tous, he brings them coffee and chats with them for a while, about women and what size breasts he likes, to regain their trust. 'I can't find anyone willing to act as collateral and spend ten days on your sofa,' Alaa says when Abu Ibrahim raises the issue again. 'I'll bring him water and food, whatever he wants,' Ibrahim says. 'I don't know anyone who'd do it,' Alaa replies again. OK, Ibrahim says. He's going to suggest something he's never done before. Alaa's friend can pay him after three days, because that's when the smugglers will be collecting from him. After three days, Alaa and the others will have long since entered international waters. 'How can we be sure that we'll be there after three days?' Alaa asks. Later that day, they find a solution. The three men will leave a friend with Ibrahim after all, but without money. Ibrahim finally consents.

It happens on the third day, around one in the afternoon. Ibrahim comes into the apartment and tells them 'It's time.' Alaa quickly buys three bottles of water. On the boat he can refill them and purify the water with tablets. They leave any superfluous clothing behind, underwear, socks, and ask Ibrahim to keep it for a while. If this attempt fails too, he's to bring their things to the prison.

A short time later, nine of them sit in a minibus. 'If I see anyone making calls,' the driver warns, 'I'll throw your phones on the ground and crush them.'

They drive twenty minutes to a park by the sea, where a young man is waiting. He instructs them to sit on the grass and act like day trippers. There are lots of Egyptian holidaymakers here, meandering through the park. The air rings with the gleeful squeals of children. Under a cluster of trees not far away, Alaa sees two young men dozing, one of them familiar. He stands up and walks over. Now the man notices him too, and Alaa recognises the youngster whose stick drove us to the beach on our previous attempt. The boy is all politeness now, telling Alaa that things went horribly wrong last time, but it wasn't his fault. The boys earn their money moving refugees from the minibuses to the main ship. 'Will it go better today?' asks Alaa. 'Please tell me the truth. My brother won't cope with that again.' The boy points to a bright dot out on the sea. 'That's your ship, it's already here. This time you won't even get your feet wet.'

The refugees wait until sunset. The last of the tourists are leaving the park. Just the Syrians and a group of young Egyptians remain. In the dusk, Alaa notices other small groups of refugees nervously entering the park, colourful rucksacks on their backs, children by their sides. Smugglers arrive too, moving from crowd to crowd and counting heads. It's almost dark, approaching seven, when one of the smugglers gives the signal. Then the groups converge and hurry towards the sea. A young woman driving through the park in a red cabriolet stops, dumbfounded. 'Where are you all going?'

'We're going on a pleasure cruise!' calls a young Syrian in high spirits. The woman gets out of the car and watches them go.

THE SEA II

That same evening, Amar sits with Rabea in a café by the Bosphorus. He has just had a shave and wears clean linen clothes that his family sent him in prison. 'What should we do now?' he asks Rabea. Having previously considered Rabea a bit simple, he is coming to appreciate his company. 'We'll find a way. Don't worry,' says Rabea. They watch the boats, often in silence, and drink tea. This exile feels almost like a holiday, thinks Amar. But the feeling quickly passes.

The refugees head towards the sea with no regard for their cover story; nobody wants to be last. They get faster and faster, soon start running, the children holding their parents' hands. They reach the shore, a small rocky terrace perhaps one metre high, a motorboat moored. The sea is calm, the boat barely rocks. They jump in, help each other, everything is orderly. None of the smugglers hit the Syrians.

'It's going well,' Alaa whispers to his brother in the boat. This attempt seems as relaxed as the last one was difficult. They have been travelling ten minutes in the growing dark when they see the second, slightly larger boat off the coast.

Hands reach out to them, hands push them from behind. The smugglers rope the boats together. There's a real danger that the

TOP: Amar Obaid with his youngest daughter and his luggage in his flat in Cairo, Egypt, on the day when he will leave his family to attempt to reach Italy.

BOTTOM: Amar Obaid, on the day he will leave his family in Cairo, sitting in the shop he has recently sold.

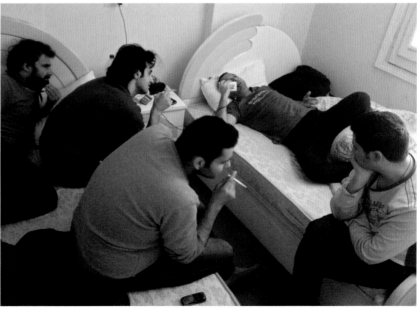

TOP: Amar Obaid counting money for smugglers before leaving his home in Cairo.
BOTTOM: Amar (second from right) phoning the smugglers, watched by the other Syrian refugees and Wolfgang Bauer (far left) in the flat they were locked inside for four days in Alexandria.

TOP: Amar (far left, his back visible) watches a gang of smugglers. (The second from the left in the white shirt is Ismail, their boss.) They have left the last flat in Alexandria and are on the way to the beach.
BOTTOM: Waiting on Nelson Island for the smugglers to return.

TOP: The smugglers' boat with refugees just off Nelson Island.
BOTTOM: An Egyptian Navy motor boat about to pick up an arrested Syrian refugee from Nelson Island.

TOP: Approaching the Egyptian Navy vessel on the small boat.
BOTTOM: On the Egyptian Navy vessel after arrest.

ABOVE: Syrian refugees on the vessel after arrest, including Alaa (second from left) and Hussan (fourth from left).
RIGHT: Syrian refugee children sleeping under arrest in Alexandria.

Bissan among the sleeping detained refugees in Alexandria.

Amar tired and desperate after days of detainment in Alexandria.

Bashar in the Milan apartment.

TOP: Hussan (left) and Alaa in Säffle; BOTTOM: Hussan (right) and Alaa in Säffle.

TOP: Hussan (right) and Alaa in their shared flat in the refugee home in Säffle.
BOTTOM: Alaa (left, at prayers) and Hussan (right, with tablet in hand) in their shared flat in the refugee home in Säffle.

TOP: Amar watches the Main river out of the window of his new flat in Frankfurt, Germany. He has finally obtained political asylum in Germany.

BOTTOM: Amar tidies his flat in Frankfurt the day before his wife and daugher arrive in Germany.

TOP: Amar meets his wife and their three daughters at Frankfurt airport. He has not seen his family since he left Egypt one year earlier.

BOTTOM: Amar, his wife and their three daughters in front of their block of flats after arriving from the airport.

TOP: Amar's wife Rolanda starts to unpack with their tired youngest daughter.
BOTTOM: Amar with his youngest daughter in their new home in Frankfurt.

boats will hole each other. Two old car tyres between the wooden hulls cushion the impact. Changing boats is the riskiest part. Refugees who make it to Europe have plenty of stories about passengers who tried to switch boats, lost their balance, landed in the water and were either drowned or crushed between the two vessels. Alaa and Hussan are separated as they get in, Hussan at the front, Alaa at the back. 'Please watch out for my brother!' Alaa begs the smugglers. 'He has bad knees!'

They speed across the water for an hour and a half. They could be arrested at any time; they're still in national coastal waters, the twelve-mile zone. They pass an Egyptian coastguard patrol boat, just a few hundred metres away. Alaa is sure it's the same one that arrested us on Nelson Island one month before. He sees men on the deck, sees the radar turning, sees them lying in wait. At least he thinks so. It's over, he tells himself, we'll soon be back in Alexandria prison. He's already searching his bag for the number of the police officer who promised to help in an emergency – but nothing happens. The smugglers seem unconcerned, and the coastguard vessel stays where it is. 'They saw us,' Alaa says with certainty. This time, the bribes the smugglers supposedly paid to the officers and crew are actually doing the trick.

'Look,' his friend Bashar says a few hours later, tapping him on the shoulder, 'the last light of Egypt.' Sitting on the stern, Alaa turns his head and sees a subtle veil of light covering the horizon. When he looks back a short while after, the light has vanished. The only thing behind him is blackness.

That night, Amar sleeps poorly in his Istanbul hotel, constantly waking, tossing and turning. He's stopped taking the Xanax, which makes it harder to sleep through the night. At some point he puts the lamp on, shoves the pillow behind his head and switches on the television with a sigh.

Just before dawn, a red flashing light appears ahead of the motor-boat. The refugees grow uneasy. They ask the smugglers about it, but no one answers. The light grows larger, rising and falling with the waves. Finally they all see it: a fishing vessel, around thirty metres in length. Their future. And possibly their end. The vessel is named *Al Basam*, 'the smiling one'. The dried fin of a large tuna adorns its prow. The boat has a twelve-man crew, most of them professional fishermen, muscular men who have been working together for years. The men on the small boat lob a rope to the prow of the *Al Basam*; the fishermen grab it and pull the two boats side by side. A second rope is thrown to the stern. The fishermen, now smugglers, help the children across first, then the women; they will take the two cabins underneath the bridge. The men stay on the deck and are carefully divided into two groups. Half of the passengers are Egyptians, who are also heading to Europe to find better jobs. When they arrive, they will claim to be Syrians. They are led to the port side, the Syrians to starboard. A few days later, Alaa will understand why.

At first the mood on the *Al Basam* is buoyant. Alaa is more relaxed than he has been in a long time; the boat seems to be in good condition and is made from metal rather than rotten wood like so many refugee vessels. There are lights, bulbs hanging in the cabins and on the superstructure. There is enough space on the deck to stretch out your legs; the boat has seventy-three passengers. Alaa has heard of other boats taking up to 700 people. Even the toilet is tolerable. The crew make them something to eat. The cabin boy, Ali, does the cooking. He hands them servings from the kitchen and the refugees pass them on until everyone has some of the flat-bread and pungent cheese. Alaa advises them not to eat, but they don't listen. Soon they start to throw up on the deck. 'Told you!' Alaa laughs.

They must be near Italy, they guess. They're wrong. Alaa thinks the worst is over. The waiting, the abduction, Nelson Island, the humiliating arrest and their helplessness in prison – it's all behind them. Wrong again.

'Where are you heading?' Alaa asks the Egyptians on the left side of the boat as he explores the ship the next day. He expects them to respond with 'Sweden' or 'Germany'. 'To Greece,' they say to his dismay. 'But we're not going there. We're going to Italy,' says Alaa. 'We're going to Greece,' say the Egyptians.

THE ODYSSEY

Alaa sees the captain on the first afternoon when he suddenly appears next to him on the bow. The captain ignores him; he rarely speaks with the passengers, and then only with the older men. The captain is called Abu Ahmed. In his fifties, small and hefty, he seldom appears on the deck. Abu Ahmed spends his nights in the wheelhouse and eats there too. The refugees who sleep nearby sometimes hear him using the satellite phone to talk to other captains or smugglers on land. He's usually swearing.

Abu Ahmed wears a dark red shirt and stained beige cotton trousers. The crew have great respect for him; a hushed command is all it takes to send them scurrying. He has left his deputy, Mustafa, to make a short morning announcement to the refugees. 'You're hungry,' he says. 'You will get food. You're tired, you can sleep in peace. If you fall ill, we have medicines too.'

Alaa is impressed by the crew, who are strong and sturdy and seem to know a bit about the sea. They come from the coastal town of Rosetta, sixty kilometres east of Alexandria. Most of them come from one family, live in the same street.

The lowest-ranking member is Ali, the cook, a lanky eighteen-year-old whose hands are rarely clean. He is the only one not from the family. He too orders the refugees around like a shepherd boy. He tells them to duck when another vessel overtakes them, forbids them to sit on the railing because it's too dangerous. He is also the one who carries the children to the toilet when the waves are too strong. The children are scared of him; his skin is darker than the others, and he smells funny too. He receives just under 100 euros for every day spent on the boat. Most of the men earn 200 euros per day.

As the journey progresses, Alaa befriends the mechanic, another Abu Ibrahim. He's in his mid-thirties, has stubble, wears a grey hooded jacket, and is a father of three. 'A good man,' Alaa reports. He is one of the highest earners, around 300 euros a day, he tells Alaa proudly. He has an assistant, perhaps fifteen years old – his nephew, Abu Ibrahim says, a nice quiet boy who's come along to learn the ropes. Like his mentor, the nephew sleeps right next to the engine. 'Don't stop praying,' Ibrahim tells Alaa. The engine is as good as new, installed just two months ago, and they have plenty of diesel – enough, he says, to travel between Egypt and Italy three times. He doesn't lie, which earns him Alaa's respect. 'I'm just the mechanic,' he says when he doesn't want to answer a question – such as whether the boat is heading for Greece or Italy.

On the second night, Alaa and Hussan come to the conclusion that if they don't reach Greece tomorrow, then they'll know they're going to Italy. A Syrian from Latakia, who once went to sea, told them it takes three days to get to Greece.

In Istanbul, Amar has started working on a new plan. Despite everything, he still wants to go to Germany. Staying in Turkey is not an option. This is not his new home. He could bring his family here, but how would they live? In this land full of refugees, where millions of Syrians and Iraqis are trying to build new lives? Amar believes it will be easier in Germany.

Implementing his plan will be complicated. Europe has sealed its border with Turkey. Western Turkey is now surrounded by high fences. Amar's attempt to flee has led him to a dead end.

Between Turkey and Greece, he would have to cross a border that follows the course of the River Evros, the shores on both sides protected by minefields laid during the Cyprus conflict (1974). The only stretch of open land is in the north, around twelve kilometres long. For many years, 90 per cent of all refugees who entered Europe illegally crossed this land bridge. It was the main escape route into the EU. More than 73,000 people used it in 2012. The Greek government decided to halt this flow by erecting a four-metre-high fence with a trench in front. They installed thermal cameras and motion sensors along the entire border. With the fence completed in December 2012, the smugglers moved to the Bulgarian border. But in 2014, the Bulgarians followed the Greek example. At their border's weakest point, they built a fence thirty kilometres long, three metres high and topped with barbed wire. The guards were given mobile thermal cameras and night-vision devices.

And so the number of casualties rose. The sections of border considered least secure by Europe's border forces are the safest for the refugees. Upgrading Europe's external borders compels the smugglers to take ever riskier routes. Every new tragedy, every new refugee who dies, is taken by the authorities as reason to make the border even 'safer', supposedly to prevent more deaths. But every new measure to shield the borders adds to the fatalities.

Amar's only choice is the sea, again, this time the Aegean.

He sits in the cafés along the street; almost all the customers are Syrian refugees. The cafés are where smugglers meet their customers, where refugees exchange news, where rumours are spread.

There are occasional raids by the Turkish police, usually without consequence. It is here that Amar meets a smuggler's assistant who advises him to fly to Izmir, where a boat will take him to Greece.

Amar agrees, leaves his hotel and flies to Izmir, moves into a new apartment, just 300 metres from the harbour with its hundreds of white masts, one white holiday yacht after another. Amar waits for a call from the smuggler's contact. Nothing happens. Finally he decides to fly back to Istanbul.

At around ten the next morning, Alaa wakes. His back is aching, his head too. Between the rolling ship and the people stepping over him, nights aren't peaceful on board the ship. Ali makes them a terrible meal, half-spoilt potatoes with rancid oil. Previously mild, the wind has begun to pick up and soon turns stormy; crests rise up before them, the boat plunging down only to be flung back up again. Alaa wedges his legs between the superstructure and the side of the ship. Many of the refugees retch and soon the deck is covered in slimy vomit. 'We're going to Greece,' Ibrahim the mechanic tells Alaa that afternoon. They will be setting the Egyptian passengers down off the coast of Crete and picking up new refugees. Then they will continue on to Italy. 'How many more are coming?' Alaa asks. Ibrahim says he doesn't know; even the captain isn't sure.

The waves get higher with every hour that passes. The ship heads for the central Mediterranean basin, deeper than the Egyptian continental shelf. They approach Crete. A strong wind blows from the north-west. The refugees' fear returns. What happens if they are arrested by the Greek coastguard? They have heard many tales; Greece is like one big prison for Syrians, a land of poverty and misery. Every morning, hundreds of asylum seekers queue at the registration office in Athens, and only a handful are admitted. The reception facilities are pitiful. Greece is surrounded almost exclusively by non-EU states, so progress is difficult. Ferries to Italy are strictly controlled, the border with Bulgaria heavily fortified. The smugglers' route via Albania and the Balkans is extremely costly. Many of the Syrians on the *Al Basam* wouldn't be able to afford it.

At around one in the afternoon, Alaa is lying by the bow when he hears a sudden crack in the air above him. 'The rope's gone!' Ali, the cook, shouts up to the captain. Alaa watches as the tender pulled behind the *Al Basam* and manned by three smugglers slowly drifts away. The crew need it to take the refugees to Italy. They don't want to lose the costly ship to the Italian navy, so the refugees will be moved into the tender once they approach the coast. A single member of the crew will then steer it into Italian waters or even all the way to the beach. Abu Ahmed's team react quickly. He puts about and his men grab the rope and pull it out of the water, soaked through and heavy as an iron chain. They manage to patch the rope and half an hour later the tender is hooked up again.

The waves break higher and higher over the bow; the water flows into the women's cabins.

Two hours later the rope snaps again.

This time the repairs take much longer; they have to replace the rope. Again they catch the tender and secure it with the new rope. After previously travelling in third gear, maximum speed, captain Abu Ahmad decides to slow down. He sounds the horn twice, the signal for Abu Ibrahim to put the engine into second gear. The captain hopes that the rope will hold at a slower pace.

At around seven that evening, the rope tears for a third time.

That very moment, the most powerful wave so far crashes over the boat. Alaa holds onto the side with his hands, pressing his feet against the door of one of the women's cabins. Children scream behind the door, many of them crying, praying to a merciful god. A few refugees talk to the smugglers, try to convince them to turn back; going to Greece is too dangerous. As nine approaches, the captain comes down from the wheelhouse and tells the passengers to be brave; they won't be venturing far into Greek coastal waters. One man cowering on the deck near Alaa asks the captain, 'How many people are you picking up there?' 'What does it matter to you?!' the captain barks.

He returns to the bridge and yells to Ali, who already knows what he wants. Ali takes an empty plastic bottle, pokes a small hole in the bottom and plugs it. Then he fills the bottle with water, stuffs marijuana into the neck of the bottle with his thumb and hands the bottle to the captain, who lights the marijuana and releases the plug. As the water gushes out, suction fills the bottle with smoke. The captain draws it into his lungs in one, two breaths. The cheapest, fastest way to get a hit. Alaa notes that almost all smugglers are constantly high; smoking is more important to them than eating or drinking.

Back in Istanbul, Amar takes another room in Best House, his regular, cheap hotel, and meets Rabea, who is now working as a subagent for one of the smugglers. Rabea has suspended his journey to Sweden due to lack of funds. His family won't send him any more money. 'I have something for tonight,' he tells Amar. He says that the bosses are preparing a large freight ship that will be sailing to an Italian port, 6,500 dollars per passenger. Amar agrees to the trip; Italy is better than Greece. He goes to his hotel, packs his things, checks out, sits in a café and waits. After several hours, Rabea calls and postpones the whole thing until the next day.

'Just like Egypt,' Amar groans. 'The same old shit.'

The moon is high, and soon Alaa sees lights on the horizon, a coastline. It's just before midnight. He thinks he can make out a chain of mountains, the boat is that close to land. Crete, says the mechanic. Abu Ahmed tells the Egyptians who booked for Greece to move into the tender. Ali and three others clean the left side of the boat vacated by the Egyptians, wash away the vomit. Dawn is coming by the time the tender returns to the *Al Basam* with seventy-three young men, all of them Kurds wanting to travel from Greece to Italy. They are thrown onto the ship by their hands and legs, like sacks of potatoes. The rough sea makes changing boats very risky. Ali tells the Syrians to move to the left side. The Kurds are miserable. They've just had their bags stolen by the smugglers who brought them here from the coast.

The next morning, after another night of dozing but no real sleep, Alaa goes over to the newcomers. He hopes Amar might be amongst them. He often thinks of him. If only Amar were here, always ready to advise, to take things in hand. But Amar is not there. The Kurds claim to come from Syria but are vague about the details and where they were born. Alaa believes them to be Turks and Iraqis pretending to be Syrian to make it easier to find asylum in Europe. 'Don't eat so much,' he advises the Kurds too. But once again, when Ali brings the bread and cheese, hardly anyone listens and almost all of them throw up. Seasickness. As the boat leaves Crete behind, the sound of gagging and vomiting fills the deck.

Even Ali, watching his culinary efforts splashed across the boards, admits to Alaa, 'It's an inhuman stench!'

On a new course now, the wind and waves are behind them, not against them. The rolling abates. The Syrians relax; the boat is back in safe international waters. They make quick progress until, the following night, captain Abu Ahmed sounds the horn once to tell the mechanic to shift down from third to first gear. 'What's wrong?' Alaa asks Abu Ibrahim. The mechanic dodges the question; he doesn't know, he just does what he's told. Mustafa, the captain's deputy, tells some of the others that they are on course for Italy but are slowing down to stop the engine from overheating.

Towards afternoon, they meet another smuggling boat from the same organisation, also heading for Italy. It needs food and water. Abu Ahmed tells Ali to throw them a few packs of bread and some containers of water.

THE STORM

That evening, Alaa notices that the sun is setting over the stern instead of behind the bow. 'We're turning south,' he says to the people around him. Bashar, sitting a little further forward, hears Mustafa telling someone that they are close to Italy, no more than twenty hours away, but the boss in Alexandria has decided that they need to change boats. They were supposed to take on 150 refugees in Greece but only half of them made it. At a price of 3,000 dollars per person, they've missed out on almost a quarter of a million, so it's not worth letting the Italian coastguard confiscate the precious metal vessel with the new engine. Now the refugees have to move to a cheaper boat.

In the night, the mechanic gives Alaa his phone number in case he knows anyone else who wants to go to Europe. If you book direct with a crew member, Ibrahim says, you pay one third less. Alaa has the feeling that Ibrahim likes him. He has honest eyes and, at this moment, he looks genuinely afraid. 'Don't stop praying,' the mechanic advises him again.

The next day, a white-and-yellow boat approaches to take the passengers from the *Al Basam*. A wooden boat. With 350 refugees it's already overcrowded. On the metal boat, Ali and Mustafa tell the Syrians to squat down, to sit all squeezed together. They threaten that if the new boat doesn't take them, captain Ahmed will hand them all over to the Egyptian coastguard. He doesn't want the captain of the wooden boat to work out how many people there actually are. But the other man is already reluctant. 'I can't do it,' he shouts across to the metal boat. He's standing on the stern. 'I don't have much space left. These are people, not animals!'

Panic erupts. A woman from Damascus begs the men to defend themselves, not to get on the other boat. 'We'll all die!' But they all know that the crew are armed. Alaa has seen a gun on the captain's map table. And what would they do without the crew, all alone out at sea? So they resign themselves to their fate.

The two boats float next to each other for a while. The smugglers on the metal ship stand on the bow and stern, the hemp ropes in their hands, tying the boats together. 'Give us some diesel first!' calls the captain of the wooden boat. 'We don't have enough diesel!' Mustafa speaks for the captain of the metal boat, demanding they take the passengers first. Abu Ahmed doesn't show his face. But the other captain continues to insist on getting the fuel first. Diesel in exchange for people. Finally the men on the metal craft throw a hose to the other boat. But the connecting clamps soon rip and the diesel flows into the sea. The two crews curse each other; yelling breaks out between the boats. Alaa estimates that this accident has cost them 20 per cent of their supply. A brown film carpets the water around the boats.

Once the hose is mended, Abu Ibrahim's pump suddenly fails. To continue transferring the diesel he needs a particular spare part that they don't have. But he knows that the ship they provided with fresh water just hours before will be able to help.

Captain Abu Ahmed goes for a risky manoeuvre. He sounds the horn three times, telling Ibrahim to put the boat into the highest gear, veers away from the wooden boat and its stubborn captain, heads towards Italy and tries to find the boat with the vital spare part. He radios the boat and asks it to wait.

After an hour, they see the other Italy-bound ship on the horizon. It has already slowed down and the spare part is ready to be thrown across. The part weighs five kilos and narrowly misses a ten-year-old child as it lands.

Abu Ahmed turns his ship around again and heads for where the wooden boat should be. Success again: after an hour's sailing they find it and fulfil their side of the bargain, refuelling the other boat successfully.

On the swell, the metal boat smacks into the wooden one and cracks the side, planks splintering under the pressure. 'You'll kill us all,' shouts the captain of the wooden boat. 'I won't do it! These are people!' He has the ropes untied and takes off at full throttle – without the refugees.

Perched with the mechanic on the hood of the ventilation duct, Alaa has a good view. Captain Abu Ahmed orders the crew to start the engine and pursues the wooden boat. Alaa estimates a five-hundred-metre gap between them. Abu Ahmed wants to force the other vessel to come about, but it dodges away again and again. Later, he finds out that the captain of the wooden boat has been calling the head of the smuggling organisation in Alexandria. Both boats belong to the same gang. The boss offers him a bonus of 20,000 dollars to stop the boat immediately and take the other 150 refugees. Terrified, the passengers start to pool their money. Their boat is old, the planks are rotten, the iron rivets rusty. They are certain that the boat will sink if even more people board. They offer to pay the captain 20,000 dollars there and then to keep going. But he tells them he has to turn around. If he doesn't, the head honchos will threaten his family in Rosetta. After an hour of negotiation and pursuit, he stops the boat.

By the end of the day, 500 passengers cower on the few square metres of the wooden boat. The population of a small village. Bodies cover the floor, legs entangled, arms pressed against stomachs and loins, belly to belly, breath to breath. Everyone's bags cement the few gaps between the bodies. 500 people, unshaven, days of dirt, vomit-encrusted clothing, the stink of urine and excrement. The mass of people at the stern pushes it low in the water. The new crew send Alaa, Hussan and Bashar to the second upper deck. It takes them half an hour to carve their way through the thicket of limbs. There is still some space at the bow, but everyone avoids it if they can; there's no protection from the wind. It's cold and Alaa soon begins to shiver. He looks out and watches the *Al Basam*. A small dot on the horizon, it soon disappears completely.

Later Alaa hears that, after unloading them, Abu Ahmed's crew cast their net, returning to fishing to conceal their true intentions. They will return to Egypt with a boat full of hake, sardines and mackerel.

In Istanbul, Amar spends his days waiting. He has taken up smoking again, getting through more cigarettes than ever. He meets Rabea in a café one afternoon. 'Tonight,' Rabea says again. But once Amar returns to his hotel – where he has now slept on every floor – Rabea calls, agitated. 'Those guys wanted to lock you in a container!' Rabea's boss, the main sales agent, declined the offer. Rabea describes how the smugglers met in a café that evening. There was an argument. 'They'll die in the container!' his boss reproached the smuggler. 'What happens if the people in the port forget about them? How are they supposed to survive for four or five days without fresh air?' They'll find a new way, Rabea consoles his friend. That night, Amar takes half a Xanax.

It's their sixth night at sea, the first on their new, nameless boat. There is no writing on the hull, and the new crew is even less helpful than the first. How different they are from the crew of the *Al Basam*. How uncertain their actions. Six skinny, gaunt boys. They are not a team, not a tight-knit group. Two of them are embarking on their first big journey. The captain, Abdullah, wears a floppy leather hat at all times. He seems more approachable, chatting a lot and clearly making an effort to form good relationships with the passengers. He even lets some of the older ones sleep on the command bridge. But he worries Alaa. He has no authority, seems more like a man amongst equals. His voice is soft and quiet, and his men often don't hear him. Would he be the right person to lead the overcrowded boat in an emergency?

That morning, Alaa wanders around the boat, it's slow-going: there are almost no gaps in which to place his feet. He teeters across the various decks, hoping to spot a familiar face in the crowd. Near the filthy kitchen, he comes across a teacher from Homs who has a smartphone with GPS tracking. To save the battery, he rarely switches it on. Up to now, the crew have assured the refugees that they are very close to Italian coastal waters. The GPS says otherwise. In fact, the smartphone puts the ship a few dozen nautical miles from Benghazi, a coastal city in the east of Libya, a long way from Italy. The teacher says that the boat is on course for Sicily, but moving very slowly. 'If we continue like this, it'll be five days before we reach Italy.'

Just after midday, they see the greenish-blue smuggling boat that provided the *Al Basam* with its spare part the previous day. It drifts on the waves. Countless hands wave to them. 'Their engine is damaged,' the captain says. He stands on the stern and makes a short announcement. 'We have to help them. We need to pull them to Italy.' The crowd becomes restless; some people call out, throw up their hands in dismay. It's only four hours to Italy, the captain responds soothingly. He assures the 500 passengers that no one from the other boat will be allowed onto their vessel. But more and more people start to shout, protesting that the boat is too weak to pull such a large craft to Italy. It will break apart, a few people call to the captain. He ought to be careful, some young men yell, adding that the six-man crew has no chance against the mass of refugees. 'There's a lot more of us than you,' they shout in utter despair. 'We'll kill you before you kill us! We'll kill you!'

The captain returns to the controls, turns and moves away from the stranded boat. Half an hour later, he heads back to it. He talks to the passengers again. He has no choice. Using the satellite phone, the bosses in Alexandria threatened to send the *Al Basam* to ram them with its metal keel. 'Then we'll all die here together.' The refugees don't know whether he's telling the truth, but this time they consent – on the condition that no more passengers join their boat.

In reality, the captain was haggling with his bosses to secure a bonus. They authorise an additional payment of 100,000 dollars. This information comes later from one of the Syrians lodged near the control room, who overheard the conversation.

And so they lash the stricken vessel to their boat.

On their seventh day at sea, Alaa asks one of the smugglers how much longer it will take to reach Italy. He says it'll be only seven or eight hours, no more. But the teacher's smartphone still places them near Benghazi. 'They're lying to us,' Alaa tells the men sitting with him at the bow. 'The GPS is wrong,' the others retort. They lie on the deck, dozing, throwing up, clutching their upset stomachs and believing that they'll soon reach Italy. Alaa has his doubts, but no one listens.

The waves grow higher again, almost as high as those off Crete. The wind blows from the front, where they mistakenly believe the north – and Europe – to be. The captain asks all the passengers to move to the left side of the boat to keep it balanced. The waves roll in from the left. Again water splashes over the decks. The children sob. Alaa watches the ten-year-old boy next to him kiss his father's hand and beg him, 'Father, don't let me die here.' Alaa also watches as the father begins to cry.

The following morning, the sun rises on the left – the wrong side of the boat – and not on the starboard like the previous two days. 'We're going back on ourselves,' Alaa tells his neighbours. He goes to the teacher, who is snoozing in the kitchen, and asks him to turn on his smartphone. The GPS also shows that they are now heading for Benghazi, not Italy. As so many times before, he asks one of the smugglers but gets no answer. Around midday, they hear shouts from the boat they are pulling behind them. They're running out of water. But Alaa's boat has little usable water itself. A thick greenish liquid sloshes around the containers on the roof. After a week and a half in the sun, algae are spreading through the drinking water.

The day passes with heavy swells. The refugees have little time to reflect; they wedge themselves in with their legs, hold on to whatever they can. Alaa can barely feel his legs; they've grown stiff with the constant exertion. Walls of water crash over the boat, toss it out of the water and send it plunging down again.

Tonight the boat reels under a magnificent starry sky. As the waves pull him from one side to another, Alaa watches them sparkle above him. He has never seen such beautiful stars. Like grains of white sugar strewn over a sheet of black velvet. He remembers the world of his childhood, a world of rich fabrics, the world of his father.

Amar calls his wife, who is impatient after a week without progress. He reassures her; he'll do it, don't give up. 'We will see each other again, Rolanda,' he says. 'Hang in there,' he tells his oldest daughter. 'I have things under control.' 'Papa loves you,' he tells his youngest, just five years old. He doesn't admit how desperate he really is. He often lies on his hotel bed, arms behind his head, staring at the ceiling.

Day breaks over the grey water. The ninth day at sea is hazy and dismal. Some distance away, they see brightly coloured luggage drifting on the water. Alaa spots an orange life jacket, then, a little closer to the boat, a plastic woman's shoe. The passengers become anxious. Some of them still believe the smugglers when they say they are nearing Italy. 'Refugees throw these things away before they take a dinghy to the coast.' That's what they say. The passengers fight to keep their hopes alive. But for most of them, this flotsam signifies death. They call to each other, discussing, whispering, praying. It looks like a refugee boat has sunk here recently. People have drowned here. In just a few hours, they'll realise how right they are.

'Just tell us where we are!' Alaa calls to the captain as he descends from the wheelhouse to go to the toilet. 'We're not near Italy! We're near Benghazi!' 'Yes, we're near Benghazi,' the captain replies gruffly, without eye contact, and walks off.

At that moment, Alaa loses any confidence he had.

They find out the truth shortly after. One of the passengers near the captain's cabin hears the skipper talking to the bosses in Alexandria on the satellite phone. He's demanding another 30,000 euros. If they don't pay his family in Rosetta in the next few hours, he'll take all the passengers back to Egypt and hand the Syrians over to the authorities. He has been sailing up and down the Libyan coast for the last two and a half days. The refugees have been kidnapped at sea. Alaa has been taken hostage for a second time.

'We might die out here,' Alaa tells his brother Hussan.

LIFE AND DEATH

The sound is almost inaudible at first, gradually growing louder. The young Kurds up on the roof hear it first, a deep humming that rises to a hard pounding. The Kurds begin to shout, waving their arms. It's their tenth day at sea, between nine and ten in the morning. Now other passengers raise their heads too. 'Helicopter!' some of them cry. 'Helicopter!' The shouts multiply. And soon they all see it. A black dot in the grey sky slowly grows larger, longer, propellers spinning above it. The helicopter circles them for two hours.

The smugglers desert their posts, running into the engine room at first sight of the helicopter. They don't want to be photographed and end up in prison. They get changed inside the boat, swapping their oil-smeared garb for clean shirts and trousers. The captain asks an eighteen-year-old Syrian refugee to take his place at the controls. 'Get away from there!' Alaa shouts. 'You don't know what you're doing.' He knows the boy; he's good-natured but slow-witted and naive. He doesn't realise that the coastguard will probably arrest him as a smuggler.

No one on the boat can make out the nationality of the helicopter. Rumours spread that it's the Greek coastguard. Despite their fatigue, some of them curse. All that effort and struggle just to end up in Greece. It's so expensive to be smuggled from Greece to Italy, so expensive to survive there. We'd have been better off staying in

Egypt, some of them say. We have family in Egypt; we could have earned money there to pay for the next crossing.

More vague shapes appear on the horizon, this time on the water. They too approach slowly. Three ships from three different points of the compass. Soon a giant vessel rears up before them, almost ninety metres high, a light blue metal wall with 'Maersk Line' emblazoned in dark blue letters. A fully loaded container ship, the largest Alaa has ever seen. Two grey naval ships approach from port and starboard, as if surrounding the refugees. The container ship turns off its engine – on the instructions of the navy, as they discover later. The freighter's bow wave would endanger the overcrowded fishing boat and might cause it to capsize. The giant ship also shelters them from the wind and the waves, forming a kind of harbour basin in the middle of the ocean. 'I wonder what's happening,' Alaa asks himself. 'This can't all be for us.'

'We are the coastguard of the Republic of Italy!' megaphones announce from afar. Some words are clear, others carried off on the wind. 'Turn off the engine or there will be serious consequences.'

In the early afternoon, Amar – still in the hotel in Istanbul – receives a call from Rabea. It's time. Rabea assures him that it'll go smoothly this time. Amar checks out and waits for a taxi in a nearby café. The driver takes a circuitous route to a modern coach that already contains fifty-five refugees. Just three are Syrian; the rest all come from Azerbaijan and Uzbekistan. Most of them are asleep. The bus leaves Istanbul and follows small roads into the mountains, heading towards the Black Sea. Amar checks their location on a smartphone. They travel through practically empty villages, winding their way higher and higher into the mountains, yet still just ten kilometres from the coast, when the driver suddenly turns around and returns to Istanbul without explanation. 'Oh, Amar,' Rabea says on the phone once he's back in Best House. A coal freighter was waiting for them on the Black Sea. 'The smugglers bribed the coastguard, who gave them a window of between two and three in the morning.' But the bus was an hour late and the freighter continued on its way.

Amar lies on the bed in his undershirt. He spends the next day making lots of calls, reviving old contacts, trying to make new ones. He discovers that Nuri – the sales agent from Cairo who arranged for his passage with Abu Hassan two months earlier – is in Istanbul. Nuri now does business in Turkey too, working across borders. 'What, haven't you made it out of here yet?' Nuri laughs on the phone. They meet at Nuri's house. He has invited two smugglers to meet Amar, Syrians from Daraa, the same town as Nuri. One after another they pitch to Amar:

'Come with me,' the first one says. They will try to get to Greece on foot. 'We'll sleep by day and trek by night.' The journey will take three days. Minibuses will then be waiting on the other side of the border. Apparently he uses this method to take groups of up to thirty refugees across the border twice a month. It costs 2,000 dollars, hiking boots and sleeping bag included. Amar turns down the offer; he has knee problems and doubts he would cope with a three-day hike.

'Come with me,' the second one says. 'You'll go to Marmaris, where we have a holiday yacht crewed by tourists. You'll sail to Rhodes with them tomorrow.' This option costs 3,000 dollars. Amar agrees. He leaves most of his things with Nuri, who can pass them on to Amar's wife in Cairo later. Everything he has fits in a waist bag. He flies to Marmaris and rents a hotel room for twenty-five dollars.

The next afternoon he meets the captain of the yacht, a Russian. His wife is there too, bouncing a baby on her knee. 'I usually only smuggle Russians,' the skipper says, but Amar looks very European so he'll take him along. However, they need good weather and his boat is just three-and-a-half metres long. At the moment the sea is too rough, the waves too high.

Once again Amar spends a lot of time lying on his bed, this time in Marmaris. For the next three days he listens to beeping cars and the hubbub of the cafés, women laughing and men smoking hookahs. When his wife calls, he doesn't pick up.

The Italians evacuate the women and children first and come back for the men the next morning. The rescue takes one day and one night. To the refugees, the Europeans look like astronauts encountering an alien species. The Italians wear white protective suits and face masks. They have plastic hoods over their heads and gloves on their hands for fear of infection.

They notice that Alaa speaks the best English of all the refugees and ask him to coordinate. Suddenly Alaa is responsible for deciding who will be next to take their final step to freedom. For so long he has had no power, been handed from person to person, followed instructions and orders. He sees the mass of people before him, calling, clamouring, begging and wailing. Everyone wants to be next, only a few show consideration for the others. He decides to let the pushiest onto the naval ships first, including the captain, then the old men. Suddenly dozens of young men, particularly the Kurds, push towards the ships; fights threaten to break out with the young Sunnis. 'Sit down!' the Italians yell. They halt the evacuation for a while, show their weapons, and the crowd grows calmer.

'You all have been so lucky,' an Italian officer tells Alaa. 'You shouldn't stop smiling for the rest of your lives.' The previous day, the Italians received an SOS call from this area. A refugee boat had capsized and was in distress. They wouldn't have been there otherwise. Alaa realises that he owes his luck to the misfortune of others. 'Yesterday I pulled corpses out of the water, two men and a woman,' the officer says, and Alaa remembers the woman's shoe bobbing on the waves.

Almost 2,000 kilometres away on the other side of the Mediterranean, the other side of the Alps, my phone rings. I am taking a short break after my time in Egypt and deportation to Turkey. It's been four weeks since I returned. I am back at my desk, working on a range of projects. I pick up the phone. 'It's over,' Alaa tells me. 'We're sitting on an Italian warship. Hussan's next to me. You should see him, he's grinning from ear to ear.'

And so it is that a reporter writing about smugglers becomes one himself.

Our laws are there to protect us, the people, and to make society better. But sometimes our laws endanger people's lives and make society worse. Should we then comply with these laws? When we were in prison, Stanislav and I promised to help the brothers. 'When you reach Italy, we'll pick you up.' We want to prevent them from placing their lives in criminal hands again. To prevent Alaa, Hussan and Bashar from risking their lives again. By making this promise, we are breaking the law. We will transport people without valid entry papers or visas through Europe. Our decision has little to do with heroism; it's about maintaining our self-respect.

*

Alaa and Hussan have managed to penetrate the EU's external border, but now they need to cross Europe. On the outside, the continent has become a fortress over the last few years. On the inside, it is divided into two security zones: the south and the north. The former is protected by the Mediterranean. Like a gigantic moat it shields the refuge of the haves from the lands of the have-nots, separates the people living in safety from those in a state of war. Anyone who overcomes this obstacle is soon faced with another: the Alps. The St Gotthard and Brenner passes.

ALIAS GALAUCO CASIMIRO

Meanwhile in the Turkish holiday resort of Marmaris, Amar has lost patience with the Russian skipper, who says the sea is too rough, the boat too small. He thanks him politely and flies back to Istanbul, back to the same street of smugglers. Amar's life feels like an infinite loop. He books a cheap twenty-five-dollar hotel again. A new smuggler has been recommended to him, an Iraqi Kurd named Abu Nagin. 'What do you want?' he asks Amar when they first meet in the café. 'I don't know; what can you offer me?' Amar responds.

Abu Nagin is a peculiar fellow, a man in his forties with thinning grey hair. He has a little belly and a carefully coiffed walrus moustache. He talks a lot, in a high-pitched voice, so fast that Amar often struggles to understand him. At some point, Amar decides that this speed, this constant omission of syllables, is a ploy, a trick to protect him from fully committing to anything. Abu Nagin offers to forge an Italian identity card with his photo for 3,000 euros. Amar knows from Rabea that the forgery workshops in Istanbul sell these IDs for an average of 650 euros. 'With a genuine Turkish entry stamp,' the smuggler tells him. He says Amar should try to take a ferry to Rhodes. 'And if it doesn't work?' asks Amar. 'Then you'll pay another 2,500 euros and I'll send you to Africa.' Finally Amar agrees and gives him the money and a passport photo. The smuggler disappears into one of the many cellars along this Istanbul street, where special machines separate the plastic cover from the paper. After just a few hours he returns with an ID card. From now on, Amar's name is Galauco Casimiro.

He flies back to Marmaris, which has a fast ferry service to Greece. His second time in Marmaris. He looks for a new hotel; he has a different name now. At eight the next morning, he stands at the pier, 400 tourists in front of him. He moves closer and closer to the passport check until finally he slots his ID under the glass panel. The woman at the counter looks at it and hesitates. The smuggler has altered the date of birth from 1987 to 1967, but too quickly. There's a shadow of an 8 over the 6. The officer calls over an Arabic-speaking interpreter, who asks Amar, 'Where did you get this?' At first Amar pretends he doesn't understand but soon gives up. They pull him out of the queue, watched by the tourists, the white catamaran almost within reach.

The Turkish officers photograph him and take his fingerprints. They are friendly and sympathetic and release him that afternoon. Amar takes a fifteen-hour bus back to Istanbul and flops onto the bed in his regular hotel.

He dials Abu Nagin's number, more desperate than angry, and says, 'Son of a bitch. So. What was that you said about Africa?'

The Milan street that Alaa and Hussan are too afraid to enter, day or night, the alley where they are hiding, is gloomy and almost deserted. I park my brand-new rental BMW with an uneasy feeling. It's just after midnight. A single bar is open for business. By the door a group of drunken young guys beat up a single defenceless man. 'This is not a good area,' says twenty-six-year-old Rafik, Alaa and Hussan's brother who brought Stanislav and me here. He is the bravest member of the family, the first who dared cross the water. Last year he travelled to Italy by boat and continued on to Sweden, where he now lives as a recognised refugee and is legally entitled to travel within Europe. When Alaa called him from Sicily, he came to Milan. Rafik feels responsible for making sure his brothers arrive in Sweden unscathed.

We hurry along the street, Rafik in front, worried that the residents will spot us or the BMW will be stolen. We disappear through a door, run down the narrow steps. An Egyptian rents the apartment to illegal immigrants at an extortionate rate, 150 euros per night. He can't know we're here. Alaa opens the door and leads us into a hovel with two cramped rooms. It's the first time we've seen each other since being deported from Egypt. Alaa has lost a few kilos and seems exhausted from his time at sea. The skin hangs across his face. He's nervous. As always, Alaa shoulders all the worry whilst his younger brother sleeps.

We don't stay long, make a plan to cross the Alps the next morning. I give them the dark suits lent to me by a friend. They mustn't look like refugees, at least not at first glance. If you look a second time, you can always tell who's here illegally. The fear in their eyes gives them away.

The Sicilian police released them from the camp after just one night, like almost everyone who arrives by sea. Italy's government is boycotting Europe's asylum laws. They don't want to bear the whole burden of the mass exodus from the south. They didn't take Alaa and Hussan's fingerprints. Italy wants rid of them; it doesn't want to keep them. The train from Sicily to Milan was full of familiar faces, almost all of them Syrian, sitting in the carriages, dozing with their heads against the windows, almost all of them passengers of the *Al Basam*.

Only the captain and crew didn't make it to the train. They were arrested at the port after one of the refugees secretly reported them to the authorities. The skipper had simply been too ruthless.

PRISON II

The morning of our departure from Milan is dull, the motorways congested. The three Syrians slump on the back seat in their ill-fitting suits. We left Rafik back in the city. He's flying home to Sweden tonight. Over the first few kilometres Alaa tells us all about the boats and the sea. Hussan and Bashar fall into another deep sleep. They've had so many days with barely any rest. We leave the Po Valley and head into the Alps. I've decided to drive through Austria. The route through Switzerland may be shorter, but the border controls are a lot stricter. Gently rolling vineyards spread out around us, then steep meadows, dark forests, cliff faces. The temperature drops with every kilometre. The last of the snow sits on the slopes. Hussan wakes and stares dumbly at the rugged mountains. The twenty-year-old has never seen anything like it.

When we stop for fuel, the three refugees stay in the car for fear of aerial police units.

We count down as we pass each sign: 240 kilometres, 210 kilometres, 110 kilometres, fifty kilometres, twenty-two kilometres, nine kilometres, and then suddenly they disappear. We have crossed the border without even realising. There is no barrier, no painted line to mark the transition from Italy to Austria. 'Was that the border?' Alaa asks, irritated. The road signs change colour – we're in Austria. We exchange high-fives, take the Brenner road down into the valley to Innsbruck and at one last pesky tollbooth pay another 10.50 euros to get through, when suddenly we see an Innsbruck state police car waiting. An officer bends down to speak to us. 'Papers, please.'

I am arrested for the second time in a month. Again, they spare me the handcuffs. They search the BMW, confiscate my phone. I am separated from the rest of the group. 'We've got a smuggler,' the inspector radios to the operations centre. I am the perpetrator because I was driving. Two plain-clothes officers lead me away. I extend my hand, but they don't take it. 'I'm the one who decides whose hand to shake,' one of them growls. 'You're in some serious shit,' the other says. Silently they drive me down the Brenner Pass to the Innsbruck police department, take away my shoes and belt and lock me in a cell. They make it very clear that they consider my crime on a par with kidnapping, robbery and murder.

We knew this might happen. Austrian Aliens Police Act, paragraph 114: smugglers may be sentenced to up to five years' imprisonment – if operating on a commercial basis or bringing a 'larger number of aliens' into the country. I know I won't serve time in prison because neither of these conditions applies. But I'm still nervous because I don't know how long it will take before the Austrian police believe me.

I spend the afternoon in various cells. After the holding cell, I am moved to the pre-trial detention block. For two hours I wait in a windowless cell, just two metres by two metres, occasionally asked for personal details through a slot below the ceiling. From here, an officer moves me to Cell 46. He presses some bedding into my hands and tells me what's for dinner. Two slices of bread and two soft-boiled eggs.

What I wouldn't give for one of Amar's Xanax tablets.

Amar is now a Frenchman named Rani Kastier. The workmanship on the new travel document from Abu Nagin seems better than the first. Passport forgers prefer Italian and French IDs, which are apparently not as sophisticated as the British and German equivalents, for example. 'If you remove the photo from a German ID, the whole page immediately turns black,' Abu Nagin explains in Istanbul. The new plan is the most expensive option on offer. The VIP package. Amar has already paid him 5,500 euros, but suddenly Abu Nagin wants another 3,000. Amar's wife Rolanda has sold her diamond ring, his wedding gift to her, for 2,000 euros and sent the money to Turkey. The next morning Amar will board a Turkish Airlines flight bound for Tanzania. Then he will continue by bus to Zambia, where he will fly on to Frankfurt. That's the plan.

As they say goodbye, Rabea warns him. 'Don't do it,' he tells Amar. 'You don't know what you're letting yourself in for.' But Amar's mind is made up. He wants to put an end to all this, any which way. To reach the north, he flies 7,000 kilometres into the far south.

OVER THE ALPS

Later, Alaa and the others tell me how they were questioned individually in Innsbruck. The police bring in an Egyptian interpreter. He stays with Hussan the longest, sensing that he is most afraid. 'Tell us the truth,' the interpreter urges. 'How much did you pay the smuggler?' They all tell the truth: they haven't paid anything. 'Why are you protecting this man?' the interpreter asks Hussan. The police employee offers to personally take all three of them over the Alps to Germany – if Hussan incriminates me, the smuggler. 'I did the same thing yesterday for a Syrian family we arrested.' The Austrian police officers sit there, unable to follow the Arabic interrogation, its threats and lies.

A few hours later, a patrol car drives the refugees back to the Brenner Pass after fining them 300 euros for crossing the border illegally. The Austrians take their fingerprints but assure them that the information will not be passed on to EURODAC, the EU's central fingerprint database for asylum seekers. Austria doesn't want them either. They say the data will only be entered in the usual police system used to fight general crime. At the Brenner Pass, the trio are handed over to the Italian authorities, where the officer on duty gives them two options:

They can get on a train to Austria. He even finds them two connecting trains to Germany in which he knows that shift changes will mean no identity checks. He writes the information on a piece of paper and presses it into Alaa's hand encouragingly.

Or, he says, you can take the train to Milan.

They opt for Milan; they don't want to go over the mountains again. They call their brother Rafik, who quickly cancels his flight and picks them up from the main train station the next morning – with a new plan.

I am released towards evening because the investigators cannot find any evidence of 'commercial smuggling'. My belt, shoes and phone are returned to me. They're only doing their job, the inspectors say. Their task is thankless. They tell me how frustrating work is at the moment, how many refugees are now coming over the Brenner Pass. 'We arrest them, drive them to the border, and a few hours later they're back.' I need to sign a form confirming that I was given plenty of water whilst in my cell, and then I can go. Stanislav and I continue on to Germany, the back seat empty.

Over the next two days, which I spend at my desk in Germany, Alaa, Hussan and Bashar cover great distances: travelling by train, they cross the French border near Nice and the German border near Saarbrücken. In Italy, just before reaching France, they leave the train to evade potential checks and walk the rest of the way. There is a French patrol car at the border. The officer sees them but doesn't stop them. Rafik follows them in a taxi to avoid being accused of smuggling and jeopardising his Swedish residence permit if they are arrested. On the train to Germany, he sits in a different compartment for the same reason. Once in Saarbrücken, they buy tickets to Kiel from the machine. In France you could only buy cross-border tickets in the travel centre, and they had been worried about being asked for ID.

Hussan and Bashar sleep on the journey through Germany; only Alaa remains awake. He sees the stations for Frankfurt, Kassel, Hanover. They change in Hamburg and take the regional line to Kiel. It's two in the morning when they arrive. The platforms are empty; the only people around are drunks and police officers. The three split up so as not to attract attention. Hussan hides in the station toilet for two hours. Alaa tries to figure out the ticket machine but gets nowhere. At around four they manage to catch a bus to Flensburg. 'Don't take the train to Denmark,' advises a Moroccan who understands their situation. 'They carry out checks on the trains.' They decide to take a taxi to the last village before the border. Alaa goes to the taxi rank and speaks to the driver, who immediately spots a chance to haggle. 200 euros for the short journey. 'In Europe,' Alaa learns, 'things cost twice as much without papers.' 'Do you have papers?' asks the taxi driver, who comes from Turkey, and Alaa gives him 150 euros. As they reach the last row of German houses, Alaa gathers all his courage, goes for broke and asks the driver if he can take them to Denmark.

The driver hesitates, grows nervous. A bit more cash versus years in jail. Several taxi drivers have ended up in Danish prisons for taking illegal immigrants across the border. Having accepted money, they are considered commercial smugglers. He could simply drive the trio to the police, and Alaa would have to apply for asylum in Germany, far from his brother in Sweden. The driver demands a surcharge of 250 euros, a total of 400 euros to drive a few metres. He disables the GPS and takes the side streets into Denmark, just two kilometres away, to Padborg. 'Is this Denmark?' Alaa asks a trucker, worried that the taxi driver has cheated him. 'You're in Denmark,' the truck driver confirms. At almost six in the morning, the three men stand at the tiny station in Padborg and wait for the train to Sweden.

Immediately, they encounter a new problem.

According to the machine, Alaa's card has no more credit. He doesn't understand the instructions well enough to pay with cash. So they get on the train without tickets. This is the worst thing that could have happened, Alaa thinks. They'll be straight off to the police. He searches for the guard right away and asks for tickets, but the man is busy with on-board protocols and says he'll come to them later.

These are the final kilometres of a two-month journey, the journey of their lives. Several kidnappings, several arrests, several brushes with death. They sit on the floor of a train packed with commuters heading for their Copenhagen offices. Hussan and Bashar have found seats in other carriages so they don't look like a group. Alaa sits next to a Somalian man who wants to chat, asks him where he's from. Taking no chances before reaching Sweden, Alaa claims to be Greek. Shortly after, the guard stands before them. The Somalian doesn't have a ticket. Alaa doesn't understand the whole exchange. The guard and the Somalian argue. Clearly he's been caught fare-dodging. 'Where's your ID?' the guard asks. The Somalian hesitates. 'ID!' the guard repeats.

At this moment, Hussan walks down the corridor to bring Alaa a cup of coffee. Alaa sends him away with a twitch of his little finger. Hussan understands immediately and hurries to the back compartments, convinced Alaa has been arrested. He plans to get off at the next station as arranged.

Hussan has no phone and only a little cash; the brothers both know they would be torn apart for weeks, if not months.

Now the guard turns to Alaa. He remembers him asking for tickets when he boarded the train. 'Do you need a receipt?' the guard asks. Alaa declines and hands over 180 euros for three tickets, but receives only one in return. Clearly, the guard has long since realised that this passenger is illegal, so he keeps 120 euros for himself. Like the German taxi driver, he too exploits the refugees' situation. He's obviously had some practice. 'OK?' asks the official representative of the Danish rail company.

On 29 May, at half past eleven in the morning, Alaa, Hussan and Bashar arrive in the Swedish city of Malmö.

ALIAS RANI KASTIER

On 19 June, at three in the morning, Amar – alias Rani Kastier – arrives in the Tanzanian port of Dar es Salaam.

He's never been so excited in all of these three long months. He knows this attempt will be his last, at least for a while. His family has hit a financial wall. Aside from the car, which he left with Rolanda, their savings are exhausted. On the flight to Tanzania he puts on headphones so that no one will speak to him in French and listens to Supertramp and Electric Light Orchestra. After a few hours in the air he goes to the toilet and tears up the ticket and boarding card made out in his real name. He learns his new passport details off by heart, his date and place of birth, when and where it was issued. It's an arduous task; he keeps mixing up the new details with those of his Italian passport.

An hour before landing he takes a Xanax to block his anxiety. The world drifts away. It becomes quieter, muted, less threatening. Amar leans back.

The city of Dar es Salaam appears below him, a chaotic gleaming mass with no apparent order. The city's countless lights know no hierarchy; they are tiny, the size of pinheads, like glow-worms. Amar's aircraft descends into a completely unfamiliar city with three million inhabitants.

'Is this your passport?' asks the airport immigration officer, looking at Amar.

Amar tries to remain calm, although the whole enterprise seems doomed. The passport scanner turns red. 'Why won't it accept your passport?' the woman asks. 'I don't know,' says Amar. She speaks to her superior, places the passport on two further scanners, on every one they have. Every time the light turns red, not green. The woman takes the passport into a back office. A second officer asks him, 'Do you have another passport?' 'Why should I?' Amar responds. He's convinced he's going to be deported. But he doesn't fight, feels detached from the situation. The Xanax is doing its job. They ask for his boarding card. He says he threw it away on the plane. 'Ça va?' the officer suddenly asks him in French. 'Ça va bien,' Amar replies. 'Parlez français?' It's pretty much all the French Amar knows, but the officer seems satisfied. The female officer returns with his passport and scans it again. Another red light. Exasperated, she enters the details into the computer and waves him through.

Amar's journey to Europe has had many moments where everything changed, seconds that reversed his destiny. This is another of those moments. For the first time, it's a good thing.

Still bewildered by his luck, Amar walks into the arrivals hall and sees a young man in a red T-shirt bearing the number 166. In Istanbul, he was told to keep an eye out for this T-shirt. Ali is Amar's bridge to Germany, although he'll begin by continuing in the opposite direction. Every two weeks, Ali smuggles Middle Eastern refugees from Tanzania to Zambia.

From now on, the boy in the red T-shirt will be his personal guide. He takes him to a hotel for the night and later, after a few hours' sleep, to a bus station. Ali has tickets for the overland bus that makes daily journeys between Dar es Salaam and the Zambian border. This time, Ali has one other customer. Amar sits down next to Abu Seif, a fat, tall Iraqi businessman who wants to enter Belgium illegally. Amar wonders how he's planning to do it. He's travelling on a forged Greek passport but speaks no Greek whatsoever and only a few scraps of English. The journey will take twenty-one hours. They drive out of the savannah into majestic mountain landscapes. National parks line the route. Amar sees monkeys on the road.

The Iraqi's corpulent body squashes Amar's legs. His hips are hurting. For the fourth night in a row he doesn't sleep. At the border with Zambia, Amar's passport makes the scanner flash red again. Again, the officer assumes there's a technical glitch and enters his details manually. Abu Seif is held at the border station because when asked where he lives in Greece, he babbles something about 'Hellinai'. Amar has tried to teach him the word 'Athens' many times throughout the journey. He's irritated by the Iraqi's stupidity. Afraid, he decides to continue by taxi alone. He's come so far, there's no way a dim-witted Iraqi is going to ruin things now. But the border officers are generous and release even the peculiar Greek after two hours.

Lusaka, the capital of Zambia, a peaceful African refuge and their preliminary destination. Smaller than Dar es Salaam, with lots of greenery, lots of parks, and skyscrapers from the sixties rising in the centre. Amar takes to the city immediately. He likes its cleanliness. In a mid-range hotel they meet Mahmoud, partner to the smuggler Abu Nagin in Istanbul. They run the business in tandem. An Iraqi Kurd, Mahmoud moved to Zambia two years ago for the smuggling business. In the next few days, Amar is set to fly from Lusaka to Germany on an African airline. Mahmoud has bribed the passport officers at the airport. They talk in the hotel's courtyard, which is filled with tropical plants. 'Give me the passport,' Mahmoud says. 'Why?' Amar asks. 'I need to book your flight,' Mahmoud replies.

What Amar receives the next morning is neither a ticket nor a reservation. Instead, Mahmoud demands another 2,500 euros; otherwise he'll keep the passport and won't be able to protect him in Zambia. Amar refuses, realising with anger that, essentially, this is another ransom demand.

ELYSIUM I

In the refugee hostel in Säffle, Sweden, Hussan performs his morning ritual of leaning out of the window to feed the seagulls. 'Look,' he says to me. 'You're not looking,' he repeats. He flings a piece of flatbread into the air. There are soft white clouds in the sky and vapour trails slicing through the blue. The bread rises, hovers for a moment, before dropping towards the courtyard where the Somalian refugees' children play football. A large gull lunges for the bread in the air, another gull attacks it. Five, six other gulls take to the wing. The bread falls on the asphalt by the entrance to Hussan and Alaa's new apartment. The gulls continue fighting, pecking and crying, until one flies off with the bread. 'What a spectacle!' Hussan beams. He loves doing this when he wakes each morning.

The brothers have no need to hide any more, not from the police, not from informers and not from nosy neighbours. They have applied for asylum in Sweden, provided fingerprints, been registered by the state bureaucracy that turns illegal immigrants into legal citizens with the right to vote. Because their brother Rafik has been living in the small town for a year now, they were allowed to leave the initial reception facility near Malmö after just a few days and move into an apartment in Säffle's Vintergatan refugee hostel. Two red-brick blocks, each four floors, face each other at the edge of the settlement. Five pine trees grow between the two buildings. 'It's all behind us now,' says Alaa, who seems more rested and relaxed, but still not happy.

Their new home is surrounded by forest, hundreds of kilometres of nothing but forests and lakes, trees and moss – untamed nature. They are big-city boys. They grew up in the centre of a city that was once one of the busiest in the Middle East. Since arriving, Alaa and Hussan have not ventured into the forest at all. And so all that remains is Säffle, a small town of 8,900 residents, hardly any of them out on the streets. Alaa and Hussan walk along deserted roads as if through an empty film set.

Whenever they leave the apartment, Hussan takes his new tablet device and Alaa takes his phone. 'Don't leave anything in the apartment,' says Alaa. 'Not everyone there is good.' He avoids contact with the other refugees in the hostel, even the Iraqi who shares their apartment and spends most of the day lying in bed, surfing the internet. Alaa speaks to him only when absolutely necessary. He doesn't want to make any mistakes; he doesn't know the rules. Alaa doesn't want to say anything that could be used against him later, although he doesn't actually know what that might be. Hussan has an easier time, talking to everyone, opening up much faster. Alaa envies him. Previously it was Alaa who always took the lead, who knew what was happening next, who kept going when Hussan seemed weaker, moaned and was ready to give up. In Säffle their roles are gradually reversing. Hussan is coping better in Sweden. He finds his way around more quickly and remembers where things are, whilst Alaa often finds himself lost in this tiny town.

'I'm still on the defensive,' he says.

The pair amble through the town, whose centre looks like an ornamental Japanese garden. There's a small square with a town hall and library, a nineteenth-century canal with a drawbridge, opposite it a tourist information centre where a German couple leaf through the brochures. They come here for the quiet. 'Where are all the people?' Alaa asks himself. His brother Rafik, who knows a little about the Swedes by now, recently explained it to him. This is how Swedish people live. They go to the office in the morning, work, visit Lidl or Netto, then return home and watch TV. The routine starts over the next morning. It's the same for the children, only they go to school instead. All very disciplined, no room for spontaneity or pleasure. Alaa shakes his head. 'Like machines!'

The town drunks congregate by the canal. They stink of booze and watch the two Syrians with disgust. 'No welcome!' one of them says. 'Go back to your home!' Alaa turns away, pretending not to hear. For the first time, someone in Sweden has told him he's not welcome. He's hurt, unsettled. He knew little about Sweden before arriving. The area around the refugee home is plastered with anti-asylum stickers from *Svenskarnas Parti*, the so-called Party of the Swedes, in reality neo-Nazis. They talk of foreign infiltration, say that Christianity must defend itself against Islam. That you can only be Swedish with the right genes. The largest far-right party, the Swedish Democrats, was voted into parliament for the first time in 2010 with 5.7 per cent. They received 12.9 per cent of the vote in the 2014 Swedish elections.

Sweden, a country of nine million people, is straining under the burden of the refugees. 2,100 arrived in the same week as Alaa and Hussan. In 2013, 60,000 migrants came in total, and the figure for 2014 exceeded 80,000. More people than ever in the country's recent history. Swedish society is finding it increasingly difficult to integrate the new arrivals. Ghettos have developed, their residents predominantly Arab and Somali. The number of unemployed refugees is rising rapidly, as are assaults and riots.

Alaa and Hussan knew nothing of this before arriving, but they are getting a sense of it now.

ELYSIUM II

On 2 July, Amar waits to show his ID in the departure hall of Lusaka's Kenneth Kaunda International Airport. The maroon-coloured passport made out to Rani Kastier sits in his breast pocket. The document has suffered over the past few weeks; the plastic is starting to peel off. In the last few days he has come to an agreement with his unhelpful host. Amar tells Mahmoud how much he has already paid to Abu Nagin in Istanbul – 8,000 euros in total – and that Abu Nagin has been deceiving Mahmoud too. Mahmoud listens as Amar phones and shouts at Abu Nagin; he takes Amar's word over that of his partner. He returns Amar's passport and books his ticket with Air Namibia, leaving Amar free to take the last big leap.

They let him straight through, don't look at him, don't even scan his passport. Mahmoud's connections. But his boarding card only takes him as far as the stopover in Windhoek, the capital of Namibia. This complicates things. Amar is afraid there will be another check at the gate in Windhoek.

But there isn't. No more checks. In Windhoek, Rani Kastier is once again presented with his boarding card. At this moment, he knows he's made it. As he walks across the concrete apron from the terminal to the aircraft, it's all he can do not to start running, skipping. 'Oh my God,' he thinks. 'Oh my God. Oh my God!'

At ten that evening, sitting with a friend in a Tübingen beer garden, I receive a text with a strange area code. Namibia. The message is short. 'OK.' The signal we agreed Amar would send if he made his connecting flight in Africa. For safety reasons, I don't know his exact location or which airline he's using. All I know is that he will land in Frankfurt in around ten hours. I've promised I'll be waiting in the terminal when he arrives.

'I'm here,' he says the next morning, earlier than expected. The Air Namibia flight has arrived in Frankfurt ahead of schedule. The German federal police are checking passengers at the door of the plane, but they don't check him. 'They only asked the black people for their papers,' he says. I'm still on the train, and tell him to wait in the transit area. I've agreed to help him deal with the police. He drinks a coffee and flushes his forged passport down the toilet. I have asked asylum lawyer Nahla Osman to assist Amar as well; she too is on her way. When I reach terminal 2, but on the other side of the passport check to him, I phone him. I'm close to tears and have to make an effort to calm down. 'Go now. Go to the police,' I tell him.

He has achieved the almost impossible. He has entered Elysium, Europe, which did everything it could to stop him.

As I complete this manuscript, Amar is living in a small refugee home in Siegbach, in the state of Hesse. Nestling between rolling hills, it is a village of almost 3,000 inhabitants. He is now trying to bring his family over. He still doesn't know how he's going to make a living. Perhaps open a car dealership? A shop with furniture from Bali, like his business in Cairo? Will his marriage last in a foreign land or fall apart like many other Syrian families? Is he the same as he was? Is his wife? One long journey has ended. Another is just beginning.

The Swedish immigration office has now recognised Alaa and Hussan as refugees. They want to start working soon; perhaps mending carpets, says Alaa, perhaps cooking, says Hussan. He loves to cook and even Alaa, his otherwise critical brother, raves about Hussan's culinary skills. They will learn the complicated Swedish language, though not a single word comes naturally. They will acclimatise to the northern cold, to the constant light in summer and the constant dark in winter. They'll do it, somehow, it's all down to them now, says Alaa.

Many of their friends are still on their way to the north, sailing across the sea, to this paradise of freedom and justice and, with a little luck, work. But Alaa seems sad and exhausted and bewildered. Not a moment goes by that you can't see where he really believes paradise to be: in the ancient vaults of the Damascus bazaar.

It is lost to him forever.

AFTERWORD TO THE ENGLISH EDITION

In mid-September 2014, Alaa and Hussan's older brother Mohamed died whilst attempting to follow them across the Mediterranean. The smugglers rammed his boat deliberately because the passengers refused to move to a smaller vessel. Estimates suggest there were up to 500 people on board, including 100 children. Only a handful of men survived, making it one of the Mediterranean's greatest maritime disasters of recent years.

When I was imprisoned with his brothers, Mohamed brought us food and clothing. He ran a little carpet shop in Cairo. The socks he gave me are still in my wardrobe. In prison, those socks made me feel human again, stinking and unwashed as I was.

Alaa and Hussan are waiting for his body to be recovered so that they can say goodbye. As of December 2014, none of the dead had been found, but the search was unlikely to have been especially thorough. They were not Westerners whose plane crashed into the Indian Ocean. They were illegal immigrants who broke laws to find a better future for themselves and their families, people without papers, their names unknown.

In March 2015, Amar's family entered Germany by legal means. They now live on the outskirts of Frankfurt. Every member of the family attends German classes; the daughters are taking to the language most easily. Amar doesn't know exactly what sort of work he wants. He says he'll come up with something.

After spending a year in Istanbul, Rabea is now living in Sweden. His family ran out of money, forcing him to work for the smugglers as an agent. As soon as he had the funds, he sailed for a second time and made it across the Aegean.

Bissan and her family were the last of our group to make it to Germany in summer 2015, and now live near Munich. For a whole year, her elder siblings took on casual work in Alexandria to support the family. When Turkey opened its border to Europe, they boarded a plane to Istanbul and paid a smuggler to take them across the Aegean. Together with tens of thousands of other refugees, they travelled through Macedonia and Serbia to Hungary, where a German activist smuggled them into Germany in his car.

EPILOGUE

These tender young faces. The baby faces of boys aged sixteen, some just fifteen, without a trace of hair. I see them in the videos coming out of the Syrian civil war. They wear uniforms, hold weapons, take up defensive positions, charge forward or lie dead in the dust, their limbs shredded. Beardless boys on both sides of the front. The war, now in its fifth year, looks younger and younger each year. Casualties on both sides are so high that more and more children and youngsters are needed to fill the gaps. In the First World War, this was known as 'bleeding yourself white'.

Syria has ceased to exist as a country. Now it exists only in fragments. It has crumbled into a number of small states with constantly shifting borders.

At the very start it was not today's chaos. Over the years, I have regularly travelled to the country to report for *Die Zeit*. I was there as thousands of people demonstrated against a corrupt government. For months, they would take to the streets every evening – peacefully – with nothing more than banners, and every evening they would be shot down by the regime's gunmen. I have seen these demonstrators begin to take up arms themselves, to shoot back. I have seen a peaceful uprising turn into a bloody civil war. I was in Syria when the rebels freed the first cities. I have watched the regime continuously escalate the crisis, deploying combat helicopters, then fighter jets, then surface-to-surface missiles that reduced entire neighbourhoods to rubble.

Whilst people were dying, most European governments pursued a hands-off policy, a policy of watching and waiting. They said a no-fly zone and military intervention would just worsen the situation.

We have held back all these years because we didn't want to make things worse. And what has it achieved? Only that the crisis in the Middle East has become so bad it could hardly deteriorate further.

Hundreds of thousands of people have come to us across the sea and via the Balkans. And now the EU's interior ministers want to close the borders. None of them have resigned, despite the thousands who have drowned in the Mediterranean in the wake of their mistakes. Europe is swamped, they say; not everyone can come; instead, we need to tackle the reasons these people are fleeing. At the same time, the UN announces that one million more Syrians will leave their country. Europe and Germany cannot seal themselves off from the force of the explosion. This war will blast open every border.

The people who take the journey described in this book will not be held back by decrees. The decision on whether these people come is no longer down to the governments in London, Paris or Berlin. These people are coming. The desperation driving the Syrians cannot be stemmed by barriers and fences. The more difficult we make it, the more people will die. But the Syrians will not be held back. There is only one way to stop them: shoot them. But even France's Front National cannot bring itself to go that far.

Why are these people fleeing to Europe? Only very few are fleeing the battles, which are anything but clear. Most are fleeing the air strikes, the cause of which is perfectly clear: the bomber fleets of Assad's regime.

The people in the half of Syria no longer controlled by Assad have never stopped asking for a no-fly zone. But the West knew better. The West, including most of the EU's foreign ministers, said that a no-fly zone would only make things worse. Shooting Assad's fighter jets out of the sky would turn the conflict into a firestorm. One of the worst mistakes in the history of European foreign policy.

The Syrian civil war became a firestorm – because the West did not enact a no-fly zone. Assad's bombs destroyed the order of the Middle East. They destroyed the structures of his country's cities and villages. They sent people fleeing who had previously organised everyday life, shaped the way the people thought: the elders, the educated, the traditional village leaders. Anyone who could afford to, left. The people who remained were too poor to flee, grateful for any support from any side. Ready to run to the devil, if he offered protection.

And so Assad's bombs helped give birth to the so-called 'Islamic State' (IS). Bomb after bomb, corpse after corpse, fear after fear, Assad's air force begot more radicals. With every bomb that fell, more Syrians turned to deranged ideologies, closer to death than life. Staring death in the face on a daily basis changes a person; for them, the paradise of the afterlife is closer than an earthly existence. In its oppressiveness, IS is to Islamists what the Khmer Rouge once was to the communists. IS now controls one third of Syria and one quarter of Iraq, an area larger than the whole of Great Britain. In June 2014, on the ruins of these two states, they held an official ceremony to found a caliphate that claims a global reach and knows no boundaries. They threaten to cleanse Arabia – and, later, the entire world – of Shiites, Christians and other 'non-believers'.

If a no-fly zone had been imposed three years ago, Syria would have been spared the crazed power of IS. Hundreds of thousands of men, women and children would still be alive. Unique cultures would have been preserved. Europe would have been spared the greatest wave of refugees since the Second World War. Now, every mayor in every village in Europe is dealing with the consequences of the West's failed foreign policies.

In 2003, the US's decision to intervene by attacking Saddam Hussein's Iraq was fatal; the West's decision not to intervene by imposing a no-fly zone in Syria has been just as fatal. But all those who made these tragic errors are still in office. All those whose strategies led to the greatest disaster since the Second World War are still working on strategies for the Middle East.

Of course, Europe's politicians are not being serious in their demands to tackle the causes of the refugee crisis. They continue to talk of a political solution. But nobody in war-torn Syria wants a political solution. There is no political solution right now. Syria is still several hundred thousand corpses away from a political solution.

And now Russia's intervention has muddied the waters even further. By joining the war on Assad's side, Putin appears to have shunted aside the possibility of a no-fly zone. The West missed its chance to intervene while it still could. Syria is a slaughterhouse. The horrors of the Paris attacks on 13 November 2015 are endured by the Syrians every single awful day.

But we have never been particularly interested in the Syrians' suffering. We are only interested in our own suffering.

What kind of people are we, the Europeans, that we calmly leave our neighbours to perish? What kind of people are we, that we watch others drown, day after day? We could prevent their deaths, but we don't, because we find their lives too expensive.

What has happened cannot be reversed. But we can, in a great act of mercy, now provide far-reaching support to those who have survived the consequences of our policies.

We've done it once in Europe already. As the Balkans were ravaged by wars, we granted asylum to all refugees who could prove that they came from Bosnia-Herzegovina. We took in everyone who came to us – on the condition that they returned to their homeland once peace was restored. During this time, 350,000 people took shelter in Germany alone and, with the exception of 20,000 hardship cases, they all went back.

How much longer do we want to watch them drown? How much longer do we want to force a generation of young Syrians into illegality? To drive them into the hands of smugglers? How much longer do we want to betray ourselves? The Middle Eastern wars are changing the people of Europe too. Gradually and subtly, we are becoming more brutal. Our protection is proving our destruction. We cannot let that happen. We need to stop the wars in the Middle East from robbing Europe of its concept of humanity.

Stop forcing men, women and children onto the boats. Have mercy.

WOLFGANG BAUER
1 December 2015

ACKNOWLEDGEMENTS

I would like to thank everyone who assisted us with this journey. The wonderful Christine Keck, who forbade me to undertake it and yet let me go anyway. My friend and photographer Stanislav Krupař for his comfort. I would like to thank the editors at *Die Zeit* for their support, particularly Annabel Wahba, whose constant availability on the phone – day and night – lightened my load, and Jörg Burger, whose editorial skills are hard to beat. For his tireless reading and suggestions, I thank Dr Ulrich Stolte, whose fantasy novels will hopefully be discovered by the publishing world during our time on earth. I thank the German Embassy in Cairo for their work in freeing us from prison.

I thank Yamen Abou Oun, Issam Hanuti, Mervat Abu Khamis, Hazem Sallwra, Mohamad Bakhash and Abdullah Baltahji for their patient support during the months of preparation.

And I thank Anas Abdul Dayem and his fantastic family. I thank them in particular.

I hope they will be reunited soon.

Dear readers,

We rely on subscriptions from people like you to tell these other stories – the types of stories most publishers consider too risky to take on.

Our subscribers don't just make the books physically happen. They also help us approach booksellers, because we can demonstrate that our books already have readers and fans. And they give us the security to publish in line with our values, which are collaborative, imaginative and 'shamelessly literary'.

All of our subscribers:

- receive a first-edition copy of each of the books they subscribe to
- are thanked by name at the end of our subscriber-supported books
- receive little extras from us by way of thank you, for example: postcards created by our authors

BECOME A SUBSCRIBER, OR GIVE A SUBSCRIPTION TO A FRIEND

Visit andotherstories.org/subscribe to become part of an alternative approach to publishing.

Subscriptions are:

£20 for two books per year

£35 for four books per year

£50 for six books per year

OTHER WAYS TO GET INVOLVED

If you'd like to know about upcoming events and reading groups (our foreign-language reading groups help us choose books to publish, for example) you can:

- join the mailing list at: andotherstories.org/join-us
- follow us on Twitter: @andothertweets
- join us on Facebook: facebook.com/AndOtherStoriesBooks
- follow our blog: Ampersand

Current & Upcoming Books